The Expanding Role
of Telecommunications
in Higher Education

Pamela J. Tate, Marilyn Kressel, *Editors*

NEW DIRECTIONS FOR HIGHER EDUCATION
MARTIN KRAMER, *Editor-in-Chief*

Number 44, December 1983

Paperback sourcebooks in
The Jossey-Bass Higher Education Series

Jossey-Bass Inc., Publishers
San Francisco • Washington • London

Pamela J. Tate, Marilyn Kressel (Eds.).
The Expanding Role of Telecommunications in Higher Education.
New Directions for Higher Education, no. 44.
Volume XI, number 4.
San Francisco: Jossey-Bass, 1983.

New Directions for Higher Education Series
Martin Kramer, *Editor-in-Chief*

New Directions for Higher Education (publication number USPS
990-880) is published quarterly by Jossey-Bass Inc., Publishers.
New Directions is numbered sequentially—please order extra
copies by sequential number. The volume and issue numbers
above are included for the convenience of libraries. Second-class
postage rates paid at San Francisco, California, and at
additional mailing offices.

Correspondence:
Subscriptions, single-issue orders, change of address notices, undelivered
copies, and other correspondence should be sent to Subscriptions,
Jossey-Bass Inc., Publishers, 433 California Street, San Francisco,
California 94104.

Editorial correspondence should be sent to the Consulting Editor,
Martin Kramer, 2807 Shasta Road, Berkeley, California 94708.

Library of Congress Catalogue Card Number LC 82-84315
International Standard Serial Number ISSN 0271-0595
International Standard Book Number ISBN 87589-954-4

Cover art by Willi Baum
Manufactured in the United States of America

Ordering Information

The paperback sourcebooks listed below are published quarterly and can be ordered either by subscription or as single copies.

Subscriptions cost $35.00 per year for institutions, agencies, and libraries. Individuals can subscribe at the special rate of $25.00 per year *if payment is by personal check.* (Note that the full rate of $35.00 applies if payment is by institutional check, even if the subscription is designated for an individual.) Standing orders are accepted.

Single copies are available at $8.95 when payment accompanies order, and *all single-copy orders under $25.00 must include payment.* (California, Washington, D.C., New Jersey, and New York residents please include appropriate sales tax.) For billed orders, cost per copy is $8.95 plus postage and handling. (Prices subject to change without notice.)

Bulk orders (ten or more copies) of any individual sourcebook are available at the following discounted prices: 10-49 copies, $8.15 each; 50-100 copies, $7.15 each; over 100 copies, *inquire.* Sales tax and postage and handling charges apply as for single copy orders.

To ensure correct and prompt delivery, all orders must give either the *name of an individual* or an *official purchase order number.* Please submit your order as follows:

Subscriptions: specify series and subscription year.
Single Copies: specify sourcebook code and issue number (such as, HE8).

Mail orders for United States and Possessions, Latin America, Canada, Japan, Australia, and New Zealand to:
Jossey-Bass Inc., Publishers
433 California Street
San Francisco, California 94104

Mail orders for all other parts of the world to:
Jossey-Bass Limited
28 Banner Street
London EC1Y 8QE

New Directions for Higher Education Series
Martin Kramer, *Editor-in-Chief*

Contents

Editors' Notes

The emergence of new communications technologies in the 1950s and 1960s convinced technology producers and enthusiasts that education would be revolutionized. Many thought that educational technology would alter the educational process in fundamental ways, making it more cost-effective, more individualized, and more accessible to those not able to participate in classroom-based instruction. Nevertheless, while millions of dollars were spent on hardware at all levels of the educational system, and while television, film, radio, and computers were used increasingly to supplement classroom instruction or to extend instruction to off-campus audiences, one could hardly call the resulting changes revolutionary. The new technologies made their way rather quietly into educational institutions—often against a good deal of resistance from faculty and staff.

But a variety of forces have combined in the last decade to create in the 1980s what it may be appropriate to call a revolution in the use of communications technologies in education. What is most discussed, of course, is the variety and flexibility of the technologies that can now be applied in instruction, administration, and research—the increased programming capacity provided by cable television; the potential of satellite teleconferencing for savings in travel costs; and the promise of teletext, videotext, videodisk, microcomputer networks, and low-power television, individually and in combination. Increasingly, educators see that these technologies can not only get the job of education done; they can train students to live in a society where, according to Meek (1983), satellite firms could provide between 22,000 and 48,000 channels for television, voice, and other communications by the year 2000. Moreover, while some $30 billion was spent on communications technology in 1980, this figure is expected to reach $150 billion by 1990.

Whether Meek's predictions of technological capacity have meaning or relevance to the educational enterprise or not, the fact is that an increasing number of people today believe that they do. Clearly, more and more educators are aware that an increasing percentage of the American work force will be employed in information and related service industries. Some estimates place the proportion at 67 percent by the year 2000. Because these educators recognize the need to prepare students for the changing job market, they are committed to the use of telecommunications technologies in education. Even more important, they are increasingly in a position to influence institutional policy.

The tremendous investment by hardware and software producers in marketing the technologies to educators has also helped to convince institutional policy makers of the need to pay serious attention to technology—and to spend more money on it. Equally important, increasing numbers of students who are

1

both sophisticated about and fascinated with technology are coming to colleges and universities.

The rapid expansion of telecommunications in higher education involves some other forces as well. As Hechinger (1980) points out, new technologies are more accepted today in part because of the experiments of the 1950s, 1960s, and 1970s: the early use of television tapes in biology learning laboratories at Purdue University; the use of closed-circuit television in medical schools to allow students to see close-ups of surgical procedures; and continuing education programs, such as New York University's "Sunrise Semester," that broadcast courses over commercial stations. These and hundreds of other projects using video, audio, and computer technology led to the purchase of vast amounts of hardware and to the employment of specialists to maintain and promote it. In most institutions, much of that hardware is still in place, and it is used extensively. For example, the Higher Education Utilization Study (Dirr and others, 1981) found that 71 percent of the 2,993 colleges and universities surveyed in the 1978–79 academic year made use of television, and 61 percent used it for instruction. Further, newer technologies, such as videocassette recorders, which are both portable and free of the rigidity of broadcast schedules, are (Rice, 1980, p. 20) "giving fresh life" to the use of television in educational institutions. For example, a faculty member can play back a videotape of a television program in the classroom at a convenient time, without the help of a technology specialist. Microcomputers, too, are portable, free of the scheduling limitations of mainframes and minicomputers, and relatively independent of technology specialists for operation and maintenance.

The economic climate in higher education has been another factor in the increase of interest in telecommunications. Now that many colleges and universities are facing level or declining enrollment and a shrinking resource base, cost-effectiveness has become an extremely important incentive. For users, the cost of hardware is plummeting. As Kressel (1983, p. 15) notes, "in 1965, the annual rental charge for an international voice satellite link was $32,000. In 1979, the charge was $5,760 (in 1979 dollars)." The same phenomenon is occurring with personal computers, videocassette recorders, and videodisk players. Many colleges and universities have cut their costs even more by forming consortia for the lease and purchase of equipment, courses, and software. For example EDUCOM is a national consortium of colleges that offers a number of services, including discounts on computer hardware and software.

In an era of declining resources for higher education, many colleges and universities are turning to telecommunications for another reason: to reach adult learners, the most promising of the new student markets. Colleges have recognized that adult learners (those beyond the eighteen to twenty-two-year-old age range of the traditional student) already constitute more than 40 percent of college enrollments. In fact, the National Center for Education Statistics estimates that part-time students will comprise 48 percent of the student body by 1986.

As part of the search for adult students, higher education has been courting business and industry. Corporations are already avid users of technology for educating and training their employees. According to Lee (1982, p. 11), former vice-president for educational planning at Prudential Insurance Company, "academia has to be ready to create joint ventures and consortia for the development of needed courseware and find new ways of compensating faculties. . . for their services. They may have to make arrangements which would allow them to respond to requests for proposals. . . on specially developed courseware for industry." Models of this kind of collaboration between higher education and business are emerging. The TAGER program of the Association for Higher Education of North Texas uses instructional television fixed service (ITFS) and cable to offer graduate engineering and business courses to employees of large corporations at their work site. Sixteen companies in the San Francisco Bay area are working in conjunction with the College of San Mateo to sponsor on-site electronics instruction for entry-level employees, who can do their course work at any one of thirty-two computer-videotape learning stations during working hours.

While these corporations and hundreds of others are calling on higher education to develop technology-based delivery systems for educating and training employees, others, frustrated by the unresponsiveness of educational institutions, have developed their own in-house training programs and software. Further, a host of private firms and organizations is developing courseware in direct competition with higher education for the continuing education market. From management consulting firms to the American Management Association and numerous textbook publishers, the commercial suppliers of educational courseware are moving rapidly into the educational marketplace. In other words, the marketing of technologies and related software is becoming big business. One constituency advocating the movement of higher education into the telecommunications field consists of educators who realize their financial stake in the development of educational courseware. Another consists of educators who are concerned less with the financial payoff from communications products than with the need for higher education to remain a central and autonomous institution in society's system of education providers. If colleges and universities do not become active producers as well as users in the telecommunications marketplace, they argue, other institutions will take their place.

Last but not least of the forces promoting change in the relationship between higher education and telecommunications is what some have called the wild growth of microcomputers on campuses. As Marc Tucker points out in Chapter One, 25 percent of the entering freshmen at The Massachusetts Institute of Technology last year brought a computer with them. Adult, adolescent, and kiddie computer camps are popular across the country, and the production of both useful and frivolous software is rampant. The popular media are filled with accounts of the glamour and power of computers. Parents, teachers, and legislators have become convinced that computer literacy is as essential for effective functioning in society as critical thinking and mathematics are. Increasing numbers of colleges and universities, including Dartmouth, Hamline University, and Case Western Reserve, now require computer literacy for graduation. The very presence on campuses of hundreds — even thousands — of personal computers is forcing institutions to do serious telecommunications systems planning and to develop strategies for training faculty and administrators as well.

One indicator that higher education has moved beyond the stage of incidental applications of technologies to systematic and institutionwide use is that several regional and national initiatives are under way to provide programming services, teleconferencing networks, technical assistance, and information to colleges and universities. In fall 1981, the Public Broadcasting Service initiated its Adult Learning Service to provide a variety of telecourses to colleges and universities in cooperation with their local public broadcasting station. By the end of the fall 1982 semester, more than 90,000 adult learners had enrolled in telecourses offered through this service — an increase of 37 percent over fall 1981 — and more than 600 colleges and universities had participated.

The Appalachian Community Service Network's (ACSN) Learning Channel is another national distributor of video programming to colleges and universities. By fall 1982, ACSN was bringing credit-bearing and professional development programming to 241 cable systems that reached 1.7 million learners in forty-one states. ACSN also owns production facilities, from which it transmits its teleconferences for educators and other professionals.

In fall 1982, the Educational Program Service (EPS) of the Southern Educational Communications Association, a regional experiment in the marketing and distribution of instructional television programming, became a national service. A system-owned co-op established for the mutual benefit of instructional television (ITV) producers and users, EPS began its national service by distributing seven series from three major ITV producers who had a reputation for high-quality materials: the Maryland State Department of Education, the Mississippi Authority for Educational Television (ETV), and the South Carolina Department of Education.

Even the area of audio programming is active. Recently, six college and university systems formed a new national service, the Adult Learning Listening Network (ALLN). With the support of National Public Radio and the Corporation for Public Broadcasting, ALLN completed its pilot marketing effort and planning for production of its first nine audio courses for adult learners in fall 1983. ALLN intends to serve as a centralized production, distribution, and marketing organization for credit courses and for noncredit and professional development courses.

The growth of teleconferencing networks has also been dramatic. Of twenty-nine organizations offering video teleconferencing services recently surveyed, twenty-four reported post-1980 start-up dates. Several of these organizations directly serve postsecondary educational institutions. For example, in March 1982, sixty-eight colleges and universities contributed $1,000 apiece to form the National University Teleconference Network, an independent network for transmitting and receiving audio and video teleconferences via satellite. Sat/Serv, a subsidiary of the Public Service Satellite Consortium, recently established a system of interconnected satellite earth stations and associated facilities located at colleges and universities. This campus conference network will also be used for teleconferencing and for distribution of programming to network affiliates. According to Kressel (1983, p. 15), the Public Broadcasting Service (PBS) also plans to "use its own satellite distribution system to connect public television stations and the instructional television fixed service frequencies to connect stations, colleges, and other public and commercial enterprises locally to offer a variety of educational programs." This national narrowcast network would enable PBS to deliver adult education to targeted audiences.

Regional networks are emerging so rapidly that it is impossible to describe them in a brief space. Statewide audio conferencing networks for geographically dispersed populations already exist in Wisconsin, Montana, Washington, Nevada, Iowa, and Nebraska. Regional consortia in which universities cooperate with interconnected cable systems are developing. For example, in PENNARAMA, Pennsylvania State University is responsible for programming, and the cable companies are responsible for delivery and interconnection. Regional programming services, such as those offered by the Chicago-based Central Educational Network, are also becoming increasingly visible and active.

There is so much activity in fact that the Carnegie Corporation funded creation of a Center for Learning and Telecommunications at the American Association for Higher Education to serve as a clearinghouse for information about new developments in telecommunications and higher education and to help colleges sort through the maze of new technologies and programs. *Telescan,* the center's bimonthly digest, provides annotations and abstracts of articles published in more than 100 periodicals, and it reports on national initiatives as well as on programs, projects, and research efforts. Because of the rapidity with which the new technologies are becoming integrated into colleges and universities, the center receives hundreds of inquiries from administrators and program developers: What are these new technologies, and where have they been used? How cost-effective are they? How do they fit the mission of my institution? What should students in my institution know about them in order to cope effectively with society and the world of work? What organizations and agencies should I contact? How will the telecommunications revolution change the shape of higher education? Can my institution become involved and still maintain its quality and integrity as an educational provider?

This sourcebook addresses some of the administrative and policy issues raised by the expansion of telecommunications in higher education. Although several chapters refer to exemplary programs and pilot projects, the book as a whole focuses on the broad questions that colleges and universities must answer in order to prepare learners for life and work in an information society.

Marc Tucker has been working under a grant from the Carnegie Corporation to examine a range of developments and policy questions in telecommunications and education. In Chapter One, he compares the widespread acceptance of computers in higher eduation today with the peripheral use of the broadcast technologies for instruction. Providing a brief history of the development of broadcast technologies, he argues that they emerged during a period of rising resources and growing enrollments in higher education—a time in which institutions felt little incentive to alter their basic mode of instruction or their internal organizational structures. Tucker points out that, unlike the broadcast technologies, computers are not viewed as a threat to the instructional system; instead they are seen as tools that support instruction, research, writing, administration—even the maintenance of the physical plant in some cases. In discussing the policy implications of this trend both for higher education and for business and industry, Tucker is the first of several authors in this sourcebook to call for participation by university officials in the formulation of federal and state telecommunications policy.

As principal author of the Corporation for Public Broadcasting's Higher Education Utilization Study (Dirr and others, 1981), Peter Dirr takes issue with Tucker's position that use of television for instruction in higher education will remain a marginal enterprise. In Chapter Two, Dirr not only demonstrates the widespread use of television but emphasizes that, despite interest in such newer communications technologies as interactive cable and computers, the broadcast media still offer the best way of reaching large numbers of adult learners. (This point is illustrated in Chapter Three by Joseph Welling, director of the Telecommunications Center at Ohio University, who notes that telecourses are broadcast by the university's PBS station, not the cable system. Why? Cable does not reach many homes in Athens, Ohio, and it does not even serve the rural areas, whereas broadcast television does.) Dirr also discusses barriers to the use of broadcast media for instruction: lack of institutional funds and support, faculty resistance, and the cost and availability of quality courses. Yet, in spite of these barriers, Dirr concludes that the use of broadcast media can be expected to increase.

In Chapter Three, through a brief account of Ohio University's experience with telecommunications technologies, Joseph Welling, manager both of the university's multifaceted telecommunications center and of the public radio and television stations licensed to it, discusses the potential benefits to colleges and universities in using both the old and the new technologies. Pointing out that telecommunications management is relatively haphazard at most colleges and universities, he stresses the importance of the trend toward institutionwide coordination of information services. Welling also raises important organizational and institutional policy issues. For example, if institutional faculty are involved in the production of telecourses, what about rights of authorship, property ownership, academic review, and royalties? At the state level, what policy changes are needed to encourage institutions to develop television-based courses? One barrier in Ohio exists in many other states: Public institutions receive no state subsidy for extending learning to off-campus sites through television.

Ohio University's successful model demonstrates how a large and diverse institution can not only use telecommunications hardware, course materials, and consortial arrangements more effectively; it also provides encouragement to colleges that have an interest in becoming producers of programs and materials. Welling clearly advocates an active, initiating role for higher education in the information society.

In Chapter Four, Robert Gillespie, vice-provost for computing at the University of Washington and director of an acclaimed National Science Foundation study of computing and higher education (Gillespie, 1981), echoes Welling's call for institutional coordination of information services. However, Gillespie focuses on the computer explosion in higher education. How should computing be integrated into the fabric of institutions? Gillespie stresses the importance of planning and clarifying how the university's mission relates to computing; the need for developing flexible budgeting and allocation schemes for computing services; the importance of faculty training and pilot projects with computers; and the complexity of the organizational and policy issues that institutions must tackle. In particular, he emphasizes the host of questions that have emerged with the introduction of microcomputers on campus. What should an institution's policy be toward personal computers? How much personal investment should the institution expect of students, faculty, and staff? What level of support services (networks, software, and so forth) should the institution provide? Who should manage the increasingly dispersed computer system? And what does computer literacy mean at a time when increasing numbers of entering students have already had experience with computers? Gillespie describes several national initiatives now under way and makes recommendations to institutional leaders about steps that they should take as they prepare their institution for the expansion of computing into all facets of university life.

In Chapter Five, Michael Goldstein, an attorney who specializes in educational policy, examines the impact of state and federal regulations on the use of instructional technologies in higher education. Reconsidering an earlier publication (Goldstein, 1980), he discusses a variety of forces that are converging to affect the use of telecommunications-based delivery systems in post-secondary education, particularly those that serve adult learners. He traces the trends toward deregulation of telecommunications at the federal level and reregulation of postsecondary education at the state level as accreditors and

8

state authorities become increasingly concerned about the host of new noninstitutional providers of telecommunications-based instruction. Goldstein also discusses the relationship of federal student financial aid policies to these issues, how the federal push toward training and retraining for America's work force may stimulate support for telecommunications-based instruction, and the emergence of multistate telecommunications-based instructional systems that are currently outside the control of the states. Like Tucker, Welling, and Gillespie, Goldstein believes that the postsecondary education community should work with the states, federal government, and telecommunications entities to design systems and develop policies that are in the public interest.

Chapter Six provides the perspective of one national policy maker outside the higher education community. Glenn Watts, president of the Communication Workers of America (CWA), the largest telecommunications labor union in the world, describes the efforts of the CWA's unique Committee on the Future, which was created in 1981 to prepare union members for the dramatic changes that the information society has brought to the workplace. He stresses the importance of worker training and career development and the need for collaboration between company, union, public sector, and academia in the training and retraining of America's work force. Watts believes that, in today's economy, unions must offer new educational services to both employed and unemployed members, and he describes the CWA's first steps in this direction. Watt's message is extremely important for institutional leaders in higher education: Despite their different vantage points, academia, business, and labor must develop effective long-term strategies for the transition to an information society.

Thus, the authors of the chapters in this sourcebook assume that the telecommunications revolution will have a profound impact not only on our methods of delivering instruction and on our approach to research and administrative work but also on the very substance of both liberal arts and professional education curricula. That is why this sourcebook addresses the broad questions raised by the partnership between telecommunications and postsecondary education. We believe that the driving force behind the development of new programs and systems should not be simply the allure of new technology. Rather, institutions should continue to base their decisions about new ventures in telecommunications on the educational and societal problems that they wish to solve and on the learner needs that they wish to meet.

Pamela J. Tate
Marilyn Kressel
Editors

References

Dirr, P. J. "Telecommunications Can Deliver." Speech presented at College Board Adult Learning Services Workshop, May 7, 1981.
Dirr, P. J., Katz, J. H., and Pedone, R. J. *Higher Education Utilization Study.* Washington, D.C.: Corporation for Public Broadcasting, 1981.

Gillespie, R. G. *Computing and Higher Education: An Accidental Revolution.* Seattle: University of Washington, 1981.

Goldstein, M. B. "Federal Policy Issues Affecting Instructional Television at the Postsecondary Level." In M. Kressel (Ed.), *Adult Learning and Public Broadcasting.* Washington, D.C.: American Association for Community and Junior Colleges, 1980.

Hechinger, F. M. "Forty Years of Educational Technology." In *The Communications Revolution and the Education of Americans.* New Rochelle, N.Y.: Change Magazine Press, 1980.

Kressel, M. "Higher Education and Telecommunications: What's Happening?" *Electronic Education,* 1983, *2* (5), 15–16.

Lee, C. B. T. "Impact of Telecommunications on Human Resource Development in Industry and the Resulting Requirements for Continuing and Higher Education." Speech prepared in March 1982.

Meek, E. "Making Room for New Technologies." *Telescan,* 1983, *1* (10), 1, 10.

Rice, M. "From 'The Ascent of Man' to What?" In *The Communications Revolution and the Education of Americans.* New Rochelle, N.Y.: Change Magazine Press, 1980.

Pamela J. Tate is associate director of the Compact for Lifelong Educational Opportunities (CLEO), a consortium of colleges and universities in Philadelphia, and needs assessment consultant to the Adult Learning Listening Network, a new organization supported by National Public Radio and the Corporation for Public Broadcasting. Former assistant vice-chancellor for alternative and continuing education at the State University of New York, she is currently a member of the board of trustees of the Council for the Advancement of Experiential Learning (CAEL).

Marilyn Kressel is director of the American Association for Higher Education's Center for Learning and Telecommunications. Before assuming this position, she was director of the Adult Learning and Public Broadcasting Project at the American Association of Community and Junior Colleges, where she worked to foster collaborative relationships between two-year colleges and the public broadcasting stations.

The incentives facing higher education in the years ahead may change dramatically the way in which telecommunications are used on our campuses.

The Turning Point: Telecommunications and Higher Education

Marc S. Tucker

The post–World War II period in the United States has until quite recently been marked by extraordinary growth in education. The group of people between the ages of five and twenty-two was increasing as a proportion of the whole population, and that group's rate of participation in education was also increasing. The capacity of the educational institutions, though growing rapidly, lagged behind the overall demand.

Into this environment, instructional television was born, and radio, microwave systems, audiotape, film and videocassettes, telephone networks, and satellite services were used to address student needs. In the main, these services were used to extend the reach of education to people who might not otherwise be served. They were regarded by most educational leaders as peripheral to the core enterprise — classroom instruction of the traditional sort serving full-time students on campus. In an era of high demand and short supply, the occasional use of communications media to extend the reach of the educational institution did not threaten this function and in fact both relieved some of the pressure and provided additional sources of political support.

This chapter first appeared in the *Journal of Communication,* which holds the copyright.

P. J. Tate, M. Kressel (Eds.). *The Expanding Role of Telecommunications in Higher Education.*
New Directions for Higher Education, no. 44. San Francisco: Jossey-Bass, December 1983.

But, notwithstanding the efforts of many able and dedicated people and the many creative projects of significant value, the application of telecommunications technology to education since World War II has warranted at best a footnote to the history of education in that period. Public broadcasting stations licensed to educational institutions, for example, generally have the status of a vermiform appendix in the eyes of school superintendents and university presidents — tolerable if trouble-free, easy to cut in hard times. Instructional television fixed service frequencies allocated to education have until recently gone begging in all but the biggest cities.

It is by examining the internal operations of the education system itself that the stepchild status of communications media can be seen most clearly. Policies made by educators, rather than those made by the Federal Communications Commission, have been the major impediments to educational use of the spectrum (Goldstein, 1980, 1981). Beginning with policies made by the Veteran's Administration on veterans' educational benefits, both federal and state education law and regulatory policy have favored financial support for full-time students over support for part-time students, they have often demanded attendance records that "distance-learning" students cannot provide, and they have required a rate of progress that off-campus part-time students cannot meet. Accrediting organizations frequently will not consider telecourses. State boards of education often require that credit be given only when a licensed teacher is physically present in the classroom, thus negating any economies that might be achieved through technology. Telecommunications has tended to be used only when someone else (usually the federal government) has been willing to foot all or most of the bill and only for so long as that external support has been provided. And, as a funding priority, telecommunications has not been high on educators' lists.

Why is this the case? The product that traditional educational institutions provide is a public good whose costs are paid mostly through general taxes on the population at large. In the case of public higher education, tuition meets only a small part of the costs. Most private institutions of higher education are heavily supported, directly and indirectly, by the government. The extent of financial support can thus be described in an oversimplified way as a function of cost that is calculated by multiplying the number of students by the estimated cost per student, which is in turn calculated largely on the basis of salary costs (assuming certain student-teacher ratios and teacher class time) as well as physical plant and maintenance costs.

An understanding of these calculations is important, because they help to explain why, for traditional educational institutions, the incentives for technological innovation and the efficiencies that it brings are very weak and why the incentives to protect the core arrangements for teaching and the prevailing organizational structures are very strong. (For an analysis of public schools that has much broader application to educational institutions that receive all or most of their funding from government, see Pincus [1972].) This incentive structure can be seen to explain why telecommunications systems have been used to extend traditional education rather than to transform it, why the costs of educational technology have typically been added to rather than substituted for labor, why local funds have rarely been used to support educational technology, and why the spectrum allocated to educational institutions has so often remained unused.

The locus of education and the identity of those who provide it are changing. Traditional institutions are on the decline as measured by many indicators, but in the workplace education and training—not just training—are experiencing a steeply rising growth and expenditure curve (Lynton, 1981). A few observations on the character and causes of these trends are pertinent: First, among those traditional institutions not in decline are those that see service to the needs of business and industry as a legitimate and important value. These include a number of community colleges (in which fully half of the nation's postsecondary students are enrolled) and continuing education divisions of universities. Second, when business and industry have expressed an interest in setting up educational programs for their employees, colleges and universities have been generally unresponsive. Thus, businesses have chosen instead either to build their own education programs in house or to buy them from nontraditional suppliers. Meanwhile, despite the long touted lifelong learning movement and the greater numbers of elderly students enrolling in traditional institutions, colleges and universities are not experiencing the rise in applications that they expected from adults.

Unlike traditional educational organizations, business organizations and the nontraditional organizations from which they buy education and training have very strong incentives to achieve efficiencies and to innovate, if innovation will pay. They are happy to substitute capital for labor, if it works. They have strong incentives, unlike traditional institutions, to teach a course in ten hours instead of twenty, if the same result can be achieved. They have strong incentives to use methods that permit their students to learn when and where it is convenient for the student, not the provider. In short, these new educational institutions have much stronger incentives to use technology, including telecommunications technology, than traditional educational institutions do.

Budgeting practices are another important area of difference between new and traditional educational institutions, particularly in considering the substantial cost of creating high-quality video or computer programming. In traditional institutions, instructional budgets are not capital budgets; they are designed simply to cover the annual expenses of traditional classroom instruction. If the money required for investment in technology has to come from the traditional budgeting procedure, it may not come at all. But a business firm can use a different calculus. AT&T, for instance, spends $1.7 billion a year on education and training, and it can make substantial investments in courseware if it sees economies down the line. Some firms, like General Electric, have started to sell their graduate-level education engineering programs to other firms, creating the possibility of educational markets aggregated across firms. Such markets, large enough to warrant substantial investment in courseware, would be ideally suited to telecommunications applications. William Norris, the chief executive officer of Control Data Corporation, has spoken of the interest of the nation's business leaders in education as a "business opportunity."

In this newly competitive educational environment, some traditional institutions are making substantial changes in the way in which they do business. For example, under the umbrella of the Association for Higher Education of North Texas, the business service of the TAGER network in Texas provides a mechanism for nine Texas institutions of higher education to pool their resources to meet the needs of technology-intensive industry in the Dallas–Fort Worth area (Association of Higher Education of North Texas, n.d. *a*, n.d. *b*). At a modest cost, TAGER will provide credit and noncredit courses in engineering, computer science, and business management to employees at the work site. Courses can be chosen from the catalogue, or they can be custom designed to employer's specifications. Taped courses originate at TAGER studios or come in by satellite for retransmission to clients by microwave or cable. Many opportunities are provided by conversation with the instructional staff, both on site and through telecommunications links. The master's degree can be earned from participating institutions based entirely on course work provided by the network. Significantly, TAGER is planning to add satellite transmission capacity to its system and thereby extend its network's reach worldwide.

In summer 1981, there were about 55,000 microcomputers and terminals in use in U.S. elementary and secondary schools for instructional purposes. By the end of the year, there were more than 100,000. The industry's conservative estimate is that the number will grow to 500,000 by 1985. (These data were provided by Richard Ballard, chairman of Talmis Inc., a market analysis firm serving the microcomputer industry.) What has caused this growth? Industry market analysts point out that patterns of computer purchases are correlated with the proportion of professional families in a given school district. As professionals, these people may be haunted by a fear that their career will suffer if they do not master the computer; as parents, they may feel that, if their children master the computer, their life chances will significantly improve. The extent to which parents are playing a key role in this phenomenon is dramatically illustrated by the fact that more than 17 percent of the purchases of computers for schools are being made by parent-teacher associations and other parent groups. This rapid expansion of computer use in schools means that there is every reason to believe that computers will become a permanent feature of the school scene, with the broad and insistent support of middle- and upper-middle-class parents across the country. No parent of the fifties ever felt that his or her children would badly damage their career opportunities if they failed to master the eight-millimeter film loop projector.

They did not send their children to television camp or buy them home language laboratories. Something different is happening now.

Higher education is not lagging behind in this expanding use of microcomputers. In 1982, 25 percent of the entering class at the Massachusetts Institute of Technology brought their own microcomputer with them. A growing number of colleges now require all students to acquire some mastery of the computer in order to graduate. Campus after campus reports a virtual rush by faculty members from every department to gain access to computing facilities.

In higher education, it is not clear that the most significant use of computers will be as teaching machines. Rather, what is emerging is the use of microcomputers and terminals as ubiquitous tools in the service of a bewildering array of academic activities, from writing and editing to textual analysis of Shakespeare, from theater lighting control to creation of computer art, from analysis of Bach's fugues to the writing of original music, from bibliographic searches to the playing of chess. Here, we see the integration of the technology into the very fabric of institutional life—the exact opposite of the case in the history of telecommunications and education.

The cost of computing in higher education has risen from $221 million ($26 per student) in 1966–1967 to $1.3 billion ($135 per student) in 1979–1980 (Gillespie, 1981). Throughout this period, more than half of these costs was for administrative data processing. Given the current explosion in demand for computing resources for nonadministrative purposes, the costs can be expected to rise very steeply.

This demand cannot be met by expanding the size or number of large mainframe computers (Cole, 1981). To see why, imagine two alternative equipment configurations: a mainframe with many remote terminals and a set of microcomputers tied together in a local network, each of which is able to communicate with the others. As terminals are added in the first configuration, the computing power available to each goes down, the time it takes the computer to respond goes up, and the risk of system failure increases, as does the number of users who will be frustrated if the system crashes. In the second configuration, the computing power increases as stations are added, the failure of any one active component does not affect the others, and system efficiency is largely independent of the size of the network. But, the main advantage of distributed computer processing in a university environment is financial. Adding major components to a large central computer is far more expensive in equipment and administrative costs than distributed processing is.

What is actually evolving on U.S. college campuses is networks of networks for the transmission of data, voice, and video (Rauch-Hindin, 1981). For example, each of Brown University's 125 buildings has its own local network, and each of these building networks is tied to a backbone network that connects them all. The backbone network (Brunet) is a broadband 300-megahertz system supporting terminal-to-computer traffic, computer-to-computer traffic, video channels for instruction and security monitoring, and channels for controlling heating, ventilation, and air conditioning. Other specialized subnetworks tie in to Brunet through gateway processors that allow the networks to communicate.

These sophisticated network systems make it possible for individual users to access a steadily increasing range of facilities, from library resources to scientific data bases, from simple dot matrix printers to multifont typesetters, from liquid-cooled supercomputers to desk top microcomputers. From the organizational standpoint, one of the most interesting and ubiquitous uses to which these networks are being put is electronic mail, which is becoming the personal communication medium of preference. This is an excellent indication of the degree to which the computer and its extension through telecommunications systems are becoming embedded in the culture of higher education.

These developments do not stop at the boundaries of the main campus. Universities were, of course, principal developers and users of ARPANET, the first national packet-switching network in the United States, and they initiated EDUNET, an interuniversity network for administrative data processing. However, relatively few members of the university community had any reason to be aware of these facilities, much less make use of them. Now of interest is the prospect of a growing demand for communications links beyond local networks on the main campus.

Faced with exploding demand from students, faculty, and administration for access to computing facilities, Carnegie-Mellon University (CMU) realized that the cost of satisfying it by expanding central computing facilities would be prohibitive and decided instead on a radical experiment with distributed processing (Carnegie-Mellon University, 1983). As Douglas Van Houweling, vice-provost for computing and planning, explained to me, by 1984, CMU plans to place in the hands of virtually every student, administrator, and faculty member a very powerful microcomputer. Each of these approximately 8,000 machines will have a thirty-two-bit address, a very high resolution graphics capability, and a megabyte of real memory. Each microcomputer will provide automatic access to the CMU telecommunications network through a specially designed communications interface. CMU wants staff and students to be able to use these machines at their residence and at other off-campus locations and still have access to all the on-campus facilities through the network. CMU is currently negotiating with the local AT&T operating company and with Warner-Amex, which installed a state-of-the-art cable system in Pittsburgh, to see which of these competitors will make the best offer to provide the data links capable of achieving a megabit transmission rate.

In contrast to CMU, the University of Minnesota is a very large, multicampus organization (Adams and others, 1981). In 1979, Northwestern Bell informed the university that its central switch, which serves 16,000 telephone lines (the largest telephone system in the state of Minnesota), was reaching the limit of its capacity and would have to be replaced by 1983. A committee of high-level university officials concluded in spring 1981 that the design of Minnesota's new system should be based on analysis of voice, data, and written communications in the university, that the system should be all digital and state-of-the-art, and that it should be owned by the university and purchased under competitive bidding procedures. The capital investment required for such a system would be about $25 million.

The university was also interested in off-campus broadband communication systems, since both the academic computing center and the administrative computing center are located off campus. In 1981, the University of Minnesota became the first university in the United States to purchase a supercomputer, a Cray-1B. To be used efficiently, the supercomputer required high-speed high-capacity data links between the computing center and the Minneapolis and St. Paul campuses. But, tariffs on Bell-leased lines were higher than the university could afford, and neither Minneapolis nor St. Paul had been awarded a cable franchise, so the planners decided to obtain an overhead right-of-way from the electric power utility. The university plan assumes use of the utility poles to connect all university facilities in a four-mile diameter area, the use of upgraded on-campus lines installed earlier for closed-circuit television, and carriage on this broadband system of data, video, and voice traffic. The university expects to gain a number of things from use of this broadband network: protection from telephone rate increases (projections place costs three times higher than the owned network under Bell's private line tariff proposal); much higher speed and capacity than any alternative system could afford; savings that will accrue as the cost of line interface equipment comes down; and capability for video transmission.

The Minnesota and Carnegie-Mellon examples suggest that the computer is becoming — in some cases, it has already become — part of the core technology of higher education, an essential tool for students, faculty, and administration. Following ten years or more of steady growth, mostly in the service of administration, computing is on the verge of explosive growth owing to student and faculty demand. Economic, technological, and administrative factors are causing this growth in computing to lead directly to widespread, insistent demand for very sophisticated telecommunications services.

This demand must be added to existing college and university demand for telephone services that is surprisingly large in comparison with the demand among business users. Educational institutions are already heavy users of the telephone system, and they are likely to become even greater users. The gross budgets of traditional educational institutions exceed $70 billion a year. The 165 universities that are members of the Association of College and University Telecommunications Administrators currently spend, on average, 1.2 percent of their budget on telecommunications. The average cost of telecommunications services for domestic business and industrial firms that are members of the International Communications Association is .65 percent of total expenses. On the basis of percent of expenses, then, universities rank with airlines and financial nonbanking institutions as heavy users of telecommunications

(Sefton, 1981). Thus, it should not be surprising that decisions about such services are commanding the attention of the highest officers of these universities, not only because the sums involved are large but because vital interests are at stake.

This chapter has argued that, over the last thirty years, telecommunications uses in education at every level have been ancillary to the main enterprise, primarily as an extension of traditional forms of instruction to people who could not otherwise participate. The incentives facing educators dictated this outcome. In an environment much like that faced by regulated public utilities and in an era of rising resources with little or no effective competition, higher education institutions had little reason to change the basic technology of instruction or their organizational arrangements in a search for efficiency or markets. The telecommunications technologies involved in that era were, in the main, broadcast technologies, and the United States provided more broadcast spectrum than the nation's educational institutions could use.

In recent years, this picture has changed, in some cases dramatically. Traditional institutions of education are facing stiff competition for a declining clientele. Costs are rising faster than revenues, forcing a search for efficiencies. Adults are in fact seeking more education and training, as institutions of higher education had hoped, but many are turning to nontraditional suppliers. These suppliers face very different incentives than traditional institutions do, and they are much more likely to use technology for direct instruction when it seems to be more efficient or effective. But, the extension of direct instruction — the principal use to which education has put telecommunications technology in the past — may not be the main use to which this technology will be put in the future. Computers, proliferating both in numbers and in the uses to which they are put, are creating a burgeoning need for telecommunications services on campus and off.

Computers do not seem to threaten the core instructional technology or the structure of the institution. That is, they do not substitute for the teacher, who is the core technology. They are tools in the hands of all participants, often immensely powerful tools for carrying out an enormous array of functions. And, there is very strong cultural support for the use of computers on campus. In short, the disincentives for significant and widespread use of broadcast technologies on campus over the last thirty years have been replaced by very strong incentives to use communications technologies that can support highly intensified use of computers and related equipment.

First, those responsible for leading and governing institutions of higher education will find that, as computing and telecommunications costs rise and as the issues grow increasingly complex, the expertise of those in the area of telecommunications policy and procurement will be required. These experts in turn will need access to the highest policy-making levels. Educational institutions that do not make provisions for these connections will pay a high price in dollars and lost opportunities. Because telecommunications is a highly regulated industry at both state and federal levels, effective participation by university officials in the making of state and federal telecommunications policy will also be necessary.

Second, because efficient and responsive providers of educational services will capture increasing shares of the market, managers of traditional educational institutions will have to push their internal constituents for these institutions to achieve the kinds of efficiencies that will make them competitive with nontraditional institutions.

Third, policy makers in higher education will soon find themselves caught in a bind between pressure applied by inefficient producers on the one hand and efficient producers and their clients on the other. The former will fight for protection, the latter for free markets and competition. In a fully competitive environment, all qualified vendors, whether for profit or not, wherever their headquarters were located, would be allowed to offer whatever courses they wished, to award course credit, and to grant degrees. State subsidies would go to students, and they would be provided to institutions only if the state had an educational requirement that could be met in no other way. Under such a policy, many institutions would go under, but students might be better served.

What makes this proposal for a competitive education environment timely — it is certainly not novel — is technology, the prospect that an institution located thousands of miles from the student can offer effective education at low cost. Just as advancing technology made the justification for monopoly of telephone services obsolete, so advanced technology may pave the way for effective competition in higher education. I am not advocating that telephone and educational services be treated as if they were the same. Rather, I am predicting that there will be increasing pressure from many sources for just such policies. It will pay to think now about where these policies make sense and where they do not and why. The public interest may best be served in some instances by making room for new entrants and new technologies and in others by preserving what is best in the current system.

Fourth, those responsible for statewide higher education planning and policy functions may want to consider what steps will be needed to attract new technology-based firms to their state and to retain those that they already have. The availability of low-cost, convenient, high-quality, and appropriate education and training is likely to play at least some role in a firm's location decisions. Among the initiatives that higher education institutions could offer to such firms are the development of backbone networks to reduce the cost of telecommunications links between employers and educational institutions, capital investment for courseware development and production facilities, tax incentives for employer investments in employee education and training, and development of research parks designed at least in part to reduce the firm's cost of gaining access to the institution's educational and research services. Such parks could include local networks, and sophisticated communications facilities would provide access to international sources of education and training as well as serve other vital business functions at a cost well below that which the average firm would incur if it had to purchase these services on its own.

Thus far, higher education has been well served by the drive to increase competition in the telecommunications industry. But, there are clouds on the horizon. Rural institutions are likely to find that their communications costs will increase rapidly as local rates rise. Relaxation of the rules restricting ownership of multiple communications outlets by one firm may make it impossible for educational institutions to find more than one firm offering to supply necessary services, particularly if the institution is not located in a major metropolitan area. If satellite owners are permitted to sell satellite channels rather than hold them open for lease, educational institutions may find it hard to get satellite service. If cable operators and teletext and viewdata suppliers are allowed to continue to control both the content of what is transmitted and the transmission line itself, educational institutions may find that they cannot reach their audiences because there is not enough channel capacity, because they cannot afford what is available, or because the owner of the transmission channel does not like what they have to say.

Telecommunications policy at the national level traditionally has been made through a process of brokering among the various participants in the telecommunications industry. Recently, Congress has shown some interest in taking the views of those who use telecommunication services into account. Policy makers must come to recognize higher education as a major new claimant on the telecommunications resources of the United States, a new player sitting down beside business and government. What kind of difference this will make or should make in policy is unclear.

References

Adams, C., Patton, P., and Rell, P. "Planning for Computing, Communications, and Information Resources at the University of Minnesota, 1980–1981." Unpublished draft memorandum, University of Minnesota, December 1981.
Association for Higher Education of North Texas. *Report on Cable Systems.* Richardson, Tex.: Association for Higher Education of North Texas, n.d. *a.*
Association of Higher Education of North Texas. *TAGER Television Network: Bringing Higher Education to Your Place of Business.* Richardson, Tex.: Association for Higher Education of North Texas, n.d. *b.*
Carnegie-Mellon University. *Preliminary Report: The Future of Computing at Carnegie-Mellon University.* Pittsburgh: The Task Force for the Future of Computing, Carnegie-Mellon University, February 28, 1982.
Cole, B. "Computer Networking in Education." *Interface Age,* 1981, *6* (10), 88–93.
Gillespie, R. *Computing and Higher Education: An Accidental Revolution.* Washington, D.C.: National Association of State Universities and Land Grant Colleges, 1981.
Goldstein, M. "Federal Policy Issues Affecting Instructional Television at the Postsecondary Level." In M. Kressel (Ed.), *Adult Learning and Public Broadcasting.* Washington, D.C.: American Association of Community and Junior Colleges, 1980.

Goldstein, M. "State Licensure of Instructional Telecommunications: An Overview of a Constitutional Problem." *Telescan*, January-February 1982.

Lynton, E. *The Role of Colleges and Universities in Corporate Education.* Boston: University of Massachusetts–Boston, 1981.

Pincus, J. *Incentives for Innovation in the Public Schools.* Santa Monica, Calif.: Rand Corporation, 1972.

Rauch-Hindin, W. "Universities Are Setting Trends in Data Communications Nets." *Data Communications,* October 1981, pp. 64–91.

Scully, M. "Notes on Radio and TV." *The Chronicle of Higher Education,* June 16, 1982, p. 3.

Sefton, N. "Telecom's Big Spenders." *Telephony,* November 9, 1981, p. 57–59.

Marc S. Tucker is director of the Project on Information Technology and Education, an activity funded by the Carnegie Corporation of New York, where he studies how changing economic conditions affect both the use of information technology in education and the requirements for an educated labor force.

Although the spotlight is now on computers and other new communications technologies, colleges and universities will be slow to turn away from broadcast media, which are the only media that reach virtually all homes in the United States.

Television in Higher Education

Peter J. Dirr

Until the late 1970s, there were few systematic data on the nature or extent of the use of television for instruction by American colleges and universities. Since 1978, the Corporation for Public Broadcasting has been working with the National Center for Education Statistics and the national higher education associations to document the extent of television use in postsecondary institutions and to explore factors that are thought to affect such use. The Higher Education Utilization Study conducted in 1979 and 1980 was a milestone in that effort. The first phase of the study, a universe study of all 3,000 colleges and universities in the country, looked only at television and involved only one administrator at each institution. The second phase of the study included radio and audio as well as television and involved a sample of 120 institutions, 960 faculty members, and 1,920 students. Together, these two studies provide a wealth of information about current uses of television and radio by institutions of higher education and a wide variety of opinion about the factors that affect these uses.

The data from the Higher Education Utilization Study (Dirr, Katz, and Pedone, 1981) argue persuasively against the uncertain future for television in postsecondary instruction predicted by Tucker in Chapter One. The data that I will discuss in this chapter illustrate that a large number of faculty are actively involved in the use of television for instruction. Tucker argues that faculty members view television as a threat, in contrast to computers, which they view as educational tools rather than as complete delivery systems. While

P. J. Tate, M. Kressel (Eds.). *The Expanding Role of Telecommunications in Higher Education.*
New Directions for Higher Education, no. 44. San Francisco: Jossey-Bass, December 1983.

it is true that the use of television for instruction can require more adjustment of the role of the faculty member than use of the computer does, the data discussed here show that the role of the faculty member in television-delivered instruction remains key to the instruction provided. Rather than replacing the faculty member, television has developed as an added component to delivery systems which continue to be faculty-directed. These delivery systems include on-campus meetings with faculty, telephone hotlines to faculty, required readings and supplementary texts determined by faculty, as well as a host of other support services that enhance the outreach of traditional classroom-based instruction.

Television and Radio Use at the Institutional Level

As Table 1 shows, more than 70 percent of all institutions of higher education make some use of television. Ten percent use it only for noninstructional purposes, such as promotion and recruitment or staff development; 61 percent use it for instruction, including 25 percent that offer courses over television and 36 percent that use it to supplement existing courses.

Looking only at instructional uses (see Table 2), the greatest portion of the effort is spent for on-campus credit offerings (44 percent), followed by off-campus credit offerings (11 percent), then by on-campus noncredit offerings (8 percent). Thus, while many contend that television is a way to reach students who cannot get to campus, we find in fact that 52 percent of the instructional television effort at colleges is devoted to on-campus uses of the medium. This evidence suggests that most institutions of higher education are still using television to serve the traditional on-campus learning needs of adults. The data do not make it clear whether television is being used as a tool or as a delivery system, but review of faculty and student responses leads to the conclusion that administrators tend to view television as an instructional delivery system, while faculty members and students tend to view it as an instructional tool that supplements and enhances traditional education.

Tracking the exact number of students enrolled in courses that use television is complicated by problems of definition and by the availability of adequate data. However, as Table 3 shows, our data allow us to estimate that in

Table 1. Uses of Television by Higher Education Institutions, 1978-79 — (2993 Colleges)

Only for noninstructional purposes	10%
To supplement existing courses	36
To offer courses over television	25
No use of television	29
Total uses	100%

Note: N = 2,812.
Source: Dirr, Katz, and Pedone, 1981.

Table 2. Allocation of Television Effort, 1978–79

Instructional Uses	
On-campus credit	44%
On-campus noncredit	8
Off-campus credit	11
Off-campus noncredit	3
Total instructional uses	66%
Noninstructional Uses	
Counseling	7
Outreach	6
Promotion and recruitment	9
Other	11
Total noninstructional uses	33%

Note: N = 2,129.
Source: Dirr, Katz, and Pedone, 1981.

1979 about 500,000 students were enrolled in more than 6,000 courses offered over television. This total includes courses broadcast over the air and intended for "distance learners" as well as courses delivered by campus closed-circuit television systems or videotape distribution. While some colleges and universities make extensive instructional use of television, the modal experience was for a college to offer one course per year over television and to enroll twenty students in that course, a situation more representative of broadcast than of nonbroadcast courses. This pattern may be changing since the advent in 1981 of the Adult Learning Service of the Public Broadcasting Service (PBS). That service is providing approximately six courses each semester to 500 colleges and universities. PBS reports enrollments well above those reported by colleges and universities in 1979.

Technologies for the delivery of television programming seem to fall into four categories according to the extent to which they are used. More than 90 percent of the institutions reported using self-contained videotape units;

Table 3. Television Course Offerings and Enrollments, 1978–79

Estimated Aggregate Number of Courses	6,884
Courses per College	
Mean	9
Median	4
Mode	1
Estimated Aggregate number of enrollments	498,201
Mean	678
Median	100
Mode	20

Note: N = 735.
Source: Dirr, Katz, and Pedone, 1981.

approximately 75 percent reported using public and commercial television stations, about 50 percent reported using cable and closed-circuit systems, and 10 percent reported using satellite distribution and instructional television fixed service (ITFS).

As Table 4 shows, more than one in four institutions of higher education (28 percent) belong to a formula consortium offering or producing televised courses. Consortium membership is greatest among two-year colleges that offer courses over television (62 percent). Another 17 percent are members of informal consortia. The services most often provided by the formal consortia are program previews (77 percent), program exchanges (74 percent), and group buys and acquisition of program rights (63 percent). Three out of four members of the formal consortia expressed satisfaction with the services that they provided, and 86 percent planned to remain a member of the consortium for at least the next three years.

Institutional expenditures for television seem to be increasing or level. Funds for equipment and staff had increased over the past three years in 55 percent of the cases, and in 30 percent, they had remained the same. In 45 percent of the cases, funds would continue to grow over the next three years; in 35 percent, they would remain the same. Projected increases for equipment were greater than projected increases for staff. All evidence indicates that few institutions permanently discontinue the use of television once they begin to use it. Of those institutions not using television for instruction in the year of the survey, 20 percent had used it in the past, and 37 percent planned to use it in the future. This was equally true for two-year and four-year public colleges and universities.

These studies have identified the major barriers to the use of television for instruction at institutions of higher education. As Table 5 shows, the principal barriers are funds and support, lack of faculty commitment, and the cost and availability of quality courses. Each of these factors, the relevance of which was substantiated by faculty responses, is a serious obstacle. In light of these problems, it is surprising that television is used as widely as it is.

Data on the use of radio are just beginning to become available. These

Table 4. Television Consortium Membership by Institutions of Higher Education

Member of formal TV consortium	28%
Member of informal TV consortium	17
Total Consortium Membership	45%
Major Consortium Services Offered	
Program Previews	77%
Program exchanges	74
Group buys/acquisitions	63

Note: N = 1,824.
Source: Dirr, Katz, and Pedone, 1981.

Table 5. Major Institutional Barriers to the Use of Television
by Institutions of Higher Education

Lack of institutional funds and support	70%
Lack of faculty commitment	55
Cost and availability of courses	50
Lack of trained support personnel	45
Lack of record rights	40
Poor broadcast times	35
Insufficient advance notice	30

Source: Dirr, Katz, and Pedone, 1981.

data indicate that 53 percent of all institutions of higher education used radio or audio for instructional purposes in 1979. These colleges and universities offered a total of almost 10,000 courses involving substantial use of radio or audio, and they enrolled almost 500,000 students in those courses.

Barriers to the use of radio and audio for instruction are exactly the same as those for television—lack of institutional funds and support, lack of faculty commitment, cost and availability of courses, lack of trained support personnel, lack of record rights, poor broadcast times, and insufficient notice. Both these findings and the use patterns suggest that use of radio and audio resembles the use of television more than it does not.

Television and Radio Use at the Faculty Level

More than half of all faculty members surveyed reported using television for educational purposes either in 1979 (43 percent) or prior to the 1978–79 academic year (22 percent). Those who had used the medium for educational purposes averaged six years of use. Most who had used television for educational purposes reported having videotape playback units available (85 percent) as well as television cameras (84 percent), television receivers (73 percent color, 71 percent black-and-white), and control room and studio facilities (62 percent). Most also reported using videotape playback units (82 percent) and television receivers (58 percent color, 48 percent black-and-white). As Table 6 shows, the delivery systems most often used by faculty were self-contained videotape playback units (73 percent), public television stations (57 percent), commercial television stations (37 percent), and campus closed-

Table 6. Television Delivery Systems Used by Faculty

Videotape units	73%
Public television stations	57
Commercial television stations	37
Campus closed-circuit systems	33

Note: This study used a stratified random sample of all faculty members in the United States. The 250,000 figure is weighted to include all faculty members who used television for educational purposes in the fall 1979 term.
Source: Dirr, Katz, and Pedone, 1981.

circuit systems (33 percent). This finding suggests that telecommunications technologies are used in a variety of ways both as tools and as delivery systems for higher education.

Funds for the acquisition of television equipment are most likely to come from nondepartmental accounts, whereas funds for the acquisition of instructional programs are likely to come from departmental accounts.

Twenty-nine percent of the faculty members who reported using television for educational purposes had received formal training in such use. Fifty-seven percent reported that they had taken a college course in which television played a substantial role. When those faculty members used television in their own courses, the dominant production modes were lecture or monologue and demonstration techniques.

Even in courses in which television was reported to have played a substantial role, only 12 percent of the course hours were televised. This proportion suggests that for faculty members television is a tool for learning more than it is a delivery system for reaching learners at a distance.

The major factors hindering the use of television for instruction as reported by faculty members are shown in Table 7. Many faculty member respondents felt that the use of television for educational purposes was not readily accepted either by the profession or by their institution. Many respondents viewed their course framework as unadaptable to television, maintained that the use of television increases the work, and felt that the institutional and professional reward structures failed to recognize efforts spent in developing and using television course materials. Interestingly, faculty members saw none of their major barriers as coming from students.

More than one out of four faculty members surveyed (28 percent) reported that they had used or assigned radio or audio for educational purposes in 1979. Seven percent of all faculty members surveyed reported that they had made some use of radio or audio in an average of two courses each; an average of 27 students was enrolled in each course. Again, the barriers to the use of radio and audio for instruction were the same as the barriers for television: lack of departmental funds, unsuitability of available courses, cost of available courses, poor broadcast times, and insufficient advance notice.

Table 7. Major Barriers to Faculty Use of Television for Instruction

Lack of adequate departmental funds	56%
Programs do not meet academic needs and/or standards	49
Cost of available courses	39
Poor broadcast times	35
Insufficient advance notice	34

Note: $N = 581,000$.
      This study used a stratified random sample of all faculty members in the United States.

Source: Dirr, Katz, and Pedone, 1981.

Table 8. Major Barriers to Student Use of Television

Poor broadcast times	33%
Inadequate equipment	26
Insufficient advance notice	23
Inadequate courses	20

Source: Dirr, Katz, and Pedone, 1981.

Television and Radio Use at the Student Level

Almost all students surveyed had used or expected to use television for educational purposes during their college career. Forty-seven percent or 5.5 million students claimed to have used television as part of their college program in 1979; another 3.5 million had used television prior to 1979, and 3.5 million expected to use it within the next three years.

Slightly more than one in four students (28 percent) who had used television in 1979 had used college-owned equipment, especially videocassette playback units (88 percent) and color (44 percent) and black-and-white (39 percent) television sets. Most of the use was in traditional college classrooms (70 percent); only 29 percent was in off-campus settings. Most students who used television in 1979 reported that such use was voluntary (63 percent), that it did not constitute a substantial portion of the course (76 percent), and that the courses that used television cost the same as courses that did not (82 percent). All these fundings suggest that in large numbers of cases students used television as a tool for learning, not as a delivery system.

The major barriers to the use of television for instruction reported by students are shown in Table 8. Students did not view the use of television in courses as burdensome, depersonalizing, or an easy way to get credit. Neither did they see courses with television as being particularly more relevant and informative than other courses were. In general, they viewed courses with television as worthwhile and as appropriate for their area of study.

More than one out of three students (35 percent) reported that they had used radio or audio in some of their courses in 1979. Thirteen percent of all students surveyed reported that radio or audio had been used for a substantial portion of one or more of their courses. The major barriers to the use of radio and audio reported by students are shown in Table 9. The barriers closely parallel the barriers to the use of television.

Table 9. Major Barriers to Student Use of Radio and Audio

Lack of appropriate radio or audio courses	41%
Inadequate courses available	20
Poor radio or audio reception	16
Poor broadcast times	15
Insufficient advance notice	14

Source: Dirr, Katz, and Pedone, 1981.

Conclusion

The data from the Higher Education Utilization Study focus primarily on television and to a lesser extent on radio. Future studies will examine the roles that other telecommunications technologies—for example, videotext, videodisk, and computer—might play in higher education. In the meantime, it is clear that television plays an important role in instruction at a number of colleges and universities today.

Its importance can be expected to increase in the near future as nationwide support services reach full strength. As noted earlier, the PBS Adult Learning Program Service is currently providing approximately six telecourses per semester to some 500 colleges and universities. The National University Consortium has built a network of some twenty-one colleges and universities that use television and other delivery systems to offer complete baccalaureate degrees. The Annenberg–Corporation for Public Broadcasting Project was established in 1980 to explore new ways of providing opportunities for higher education through telecommunications. In its first two years of operation, it funded fourteen projects that will yield courses using 100 hours of televised instruction and more than 30 hours of audio and radio instruction. The To Educate the People Consortium has a network of fifteen colleges and universities that work with local labor unions to provide labor-oriented baccalaureate degrees; courses delivered over television are part of this effort. Recently, National Public Radio worked with six major colleges and universities to form a new national organization, the Adult Learning Listening Network, to develop, produce, and distribute high-quality audio and radio courses at the college level. The list goes on.

It is interesting to note that most of these efforts rely in part on a broadcast medium. This creates an interesting phenomenon that only recently has been measured systematically. As video and audio lessons are broadcast, usually at the instigation of one or more colleges and universities, they attract an audience that is far larger than the audience of students enrolled in the courses for credit. We have dubbed these nonenrolled viewers and listeners *informal learners*, and we estimate that there are often 100,000 informal learners for each enrolled student. For instance, we know that approximately 10 million persons viewed the "Cosmos" television series, one of the largest audiences for any public broadcasting series. Although most of this viewing audience was not enrolled for credit, this number of viewers is almost equal to all the full-time equivalent enrollments in higher education in 1980, the years in which "Cosmos" was first broadcast.

These numbers suggest that, if appropriate services were developed to meet the learning needs of these informal learners, the potential size of the market, both for colleges and universities and for telecommunications entities, would be much larger than anyone estimates. We do know that there are about 58 million persons in this country twenty-five years of age or older who have completed high school but who have not completed college and who are not now enrolled in college. Twelve million of those 58 million completed one to three years of college, then dropped out, while 21 million expect to complete college at some time. Using these figures, it may be possible to project a potential market, assess the needs of that market, and devise programming to serve it.

The level of audience needed to justify a program like "Cosmos" or even "Humanities Through the Arts" can only be reached today by broadcast television and radio, which are the only media that reach virtually all 78 million households in the United States. Of all the other telecommunications technologies, only cable television and videocassette recorders are expected to have exceeded by 1990 the 15 percent penetration rate that is believed to be the level at which a market becomes self-perpetuating.

A few words about the potential of cable and its current use are important here. The emphasis of this chapter on broadcasting is not meant to indicate that cable cannot offer colleges and universities a useful vehicle for serving learners. Newspaper accounts describe new cable systems that boast 100 channels, crystal clear pictures, first-run movies, instant stock market quotations, in-home shopping, twenty-four hour security, and many more services. It is easy for educators to lose sight of the fact that, of the 4,600 cable systems in existence at the time of our study, 80 percent (3,680) were six- or twelve-channel systems, which were hardly capable of providing a very wide range of services to subscribers. Even in 1982, when more than 5,000 cable systems were in operation, close to 60 percent were still six- to twelve-channel systems. Moreover, only about one in three American television households can receive at least the basic cable television service. Finally, only half of the top twenty-five television markets are currently wired for cable and have operational cable systems. While cable is not available in the other major markets at this time, it probably will be within the next five to seven years.

In spite of these low penetration levels, the Higher Education Utilization Study found that 17 percent of all colleges had used cable television for instruction in 1979 and that cable was the sole or primary instructional television distribution outlet for 163 colleges. Cable accounted for about 6 percent of the courses offered over television, and it generated about 4 percent of the enrollments in courses over television. These figures can help colleges and universities to define realistic enrollment goals for courses or workshops offered over cable. They also indicate that the long-term potential of cable for serving learners is substantial. For these reasons, institutions of higher education should begin working with their local cable operators (or with their city council if no cable system is in place) to increase educational access.

In the rush to use the new technologies, colleges and universities must not forget that, for most Americans in 1990, the use of telecommunications technologies in their private life will be more like it is today than it will not; that is, there will be "channels" that deliver entertainment and informational programming that someone else has produced. Even for the relatively small percentage of viewers who will use the technologies to learn in their own home, the technologies will primarily serve as channels to bring materials that others have designed and prepackaged, as in the case of telecourses today.

For all these reasons, many colleges and universities will be very slow to turn away from broadcast media, even as they gradually increase their use of nonbroadcast television, radio and audio systems, and other telecommunications technologies. The findings of the Higher Education Utilization Study clearly demonstrate the continuing reliance of institutions of higher education on broadcast technology.

Reference

Dirr, P., Katz, J. H., and Pedone, R. J. *Higher Education Utilization Study.* Washington, D.C.: Corporation for Public Broadcasting, 1981.

Peter J. Dirr is associate director for research and evaluation of the Annenberg–Corporation for Public Broadcasting Project. He has taught communications and education courses at the State University of New York College at Buffalo and at Manhattanville College.

*This case study shares practical, direct experience from a major
university in dealing with opportunities and issues in the delivery
of higher education telecommunications services.*

A Management Perspective

Joseph Welling

Telecommunications management is relatively haphazard at most colleges
and universities today. The computer center, the library, the radio and television stations, the closed-circuit television system, and the audiovisual center
are all likely to be separately managed. Some may be pulled together, but for
the most part they have their own roles and their own constituencies. This
chapter is written from the point of view of a telecommunications service
manager within a university who is responsible for the daily delivery of public
programs and instructional support. A good part of the attention of such a
manager is directed to the realization of daily services. Unlike advisers, who
are free to focus only on broad policy issues, service managers must have their
view of the future rooted firmly in the realities required to make the university
telecommunications complex work each day. They must know firsthand the
problems associated with encouraging new teaching and learning modes
among faculties and students. They must deal with funding shortages. They
must realize the prerogatives of the groups that make judgments within an
institution of higher education, such as the groups that make decisions about
the award of credit. They must provide environments to encourage risk takers
and creative production staff members so that a critical edge of innovation can
be maintained. This edge is essential for success both in program development
and in translation of policies and plans into the real, tangible experiences of
education.

    Future concerns and planning should also be at the heart of the

P. J. Tate, M. Kressel (Eds.). *The Expanding Role of Telecommunications in Higher Education.*
New Directions for Higher Education, no. 44. San Francisco: Jossey-Bass, December 1983.

management role. Telecommunications planning involves active participation in the development both of internal university policies or goals and of external relationships. Telecommunications managers must be prepared to help shape policies for national service organizations in a large public enterprise. They must also be prepared to engage the political instruments needed to make those policies real. A unique planning element in educational telecommunications has to do with the speed with which technological changes are taking place and with the layers of legal and regulatory issues that will shape the application of these technical changes to the interests of education. The manager's job here is to advise university administrators so that the institution can have an impact on these changes where possible and so that it can be in a position to make reasonable choices among the technological options available.

These two aspects of management are in some ways complementary. They provide a grounding in practicality at times when change is rapid and when the technical options seem almost infinite. This is a useful point of view to share with educational leaders at a time when enthusiasm for telecommunications applications is growing, as it is in the higher education community today. Interest in the use of electronic systems to support learning is quickening. Faculties and administrators are coming to feel the excitement. Students raised with electronic systems take them to be the normal tools of life.

Our fascination with the new technologies stems from our belief that they hold great promise for helping colleges and universities to address common problems and interests. This belief has been heightened by a number of factors in today's environment. One is the pressure on funding, which causes interest in cooperation among institutions to increase. Another is the change in the demographic makeup of today's student body, where individuals over twenty-five years of age make up 38 percent of all college enrollments. Institutions across the country are searching for systems to serve these nontraditional students more effectively. Still another factor is the changing relationship between the higher education community and the private sector, where the faltering economy has challenged long-standing business and employment assumptions and where training opportunities are seen as critical if American business is to maintain a competitive position. Finally, our interest in the educational use of these technologies has been stimulated by increased access to these technologies in the other parts of our lives. If cable television can deliver 100 channels of entertainment to a home, can it also be used to provide education? How can a home videotape recorder be used for something more than delayed viewing of the nightly news? The general public, including faculty, students, and administrators, has been caught up in the excitement of these new technologies and our ease of access to them.

Educational Objectives

The new technologies can help colleges and universities to respond to these opportunities in a variety of ways. First, they can provide place flexibility in addressing the instructional needs of nontraditional students by delivering course materials to their homes and places of work. Such delivery can be accomplished by telephone-system access to computer-assisted or computer-managed instruction. It can include television materials delivered on cassette that are augmented by printed study guides, telephone conferences, and campus visits singly or in combination. Audiocassettes to supplement study materials can be used by commuters while they are in transit between workplace and home. Multiple offerings of television courses can be provided simultaneously through cable channels. These services can include locally originated television programs from participating institutions as well as material distributed nationally by earth satellite networks, such as that of the Public Broadcasting Service or the Appalachian Community Service Network's Learning Channel.

Second, they can provide time flexibility in addressing the instructional needs of nontraditional learners, since these services can include frequently repeated program materials, and they can be offered twenty-four hours a day. The computer providing direct instruction or bibliographic search services for nontraditional students is as ready to respond at 2:00 A.M. as it is during working hours. Cable television educational programming can be cycled throughout the day, as it is now in the Detroit metropolitan area, where an independent community corporation operating the public television station has developed services recognizing the needs of afternoon and night shift workers. The College Cable Channel in Detroit includes five participating cable companies and four accrediting colleges that serve adult learners in sixteen suburban communities.

Third, these technologies can extend access to limited human resources. The impact of specialized faculty skills can be extended through mediated instructional material. This can be especially critical in the areas of science and high technology, where shortages of trained people are likely to continue through the end of this decade. It is also a significant arena for educational development in support of the nation's reindustrialization.

Fourth, in addition to direct support of the teaching and learning process, new technologies can provide user-selected public information about institutional programs and activities. Most of our efforts at informing potential students are carried out through traditional print promotion campaigns and advertising, which seek to provide the potential student with information at a time when it is of value to him or her. Electronic systems can provide public information of this sort through a variety of instruments: It can be incorporated in the service networks of private, for-profit information providers, such as CompuServe, where it can be accessed by subscribers using home computer terminals. It can be broadcast as a teletext service by a local public television station and viewed on home television receivers using decoders. Teletext services can also be expanded to provide thousands of pages of information by using a full channel on a local cable television system. For example, cooperating colleges can combine listings of all continuing education courses so that an individual interested in a given subject area can review all those offerings in an up-to-date list at his or her discretion.

Fifth, these technologies can promote interinstitutional cooperation and resource sharing. For example, cable television systems in an urban area can be used to link existing computers at colleges, universities, research organizations, and other public agenices for research support. Two-way, interactive closed-circuit instructional television services can be shared between institutions via cable or dedicated microwave systems. Clinical observations televised from health agencies can be provided through instructional closed-circuit systems with privacy assured for use in health training courses at participating universities.

Sixth, these technologies can provide opportunities for cost sharing and income generation. Approached cooperatively, they can be developed in such a way as to take advantage both of their multiple capacities and of their insensitivity to the traditional limits of time and place. The cost of an intercity microwave system for television can be made more attractive by adding data channels to offset long-term lease arrangements for data transmission by the telephone company. Income can be generated by increased enrollments and by the sale to other institutions of new creative work in these fields. If videocassettes made for local instructional use are properly marketed, they can be sold to colleagues at other institutions.

Seventh, the text and information services described earlier should lead to improved recruiting, especially of nontraditional students.

Eighth, some of these technologies provide instruments for linking local institutions with nationwide networks that deliver such services as teleconferencing for training and professional development. Such linkage may best be done through another public telecommunications entity, with the teleconference delivered by cable or some similar local system.

Finally, use of these technologies by colleges and universities creates a varied range of laboratory opportunities for students who are being trained to deliver telecommunications services in their academic work. As information service training increasingly involves diverse academic fields, laboratory opportunities can be created for students in related campus services. In the pages that follow, I will discuss each of these educational objectives in light of our experiences at Ohio University, treating technological, organizational, and policy concerns that have been introduced there.

The Setting

Ohio University serves about 20,000 students on six campuses in the state's Appalachian corridor. A Revolutionary War land-grant institution, its history is closely tied to that of the communities in its primary service area. Its rural environment has led the university to explore a wide range of telecommunications systems to support its teaching, research, and service roles. These systems provide contact with people in all walks of life throughout the region, which is about 200 miles long and 90 miles wide and which centers on the Ohio River. Through its main campus in Athens and five regional campuses, the university has established the core of an educational network that supports a wide range of graduate and undergraduate academic programs in eight degree-granting colleges. Noncredit continuing education services are extended throughout the region. Study opportunities are provided worldwide through the university's Independent Study Through Correspondence programs. Finally, Ohio University is an active member of the international community with programs in Asia, Africa, Europe, and South America. During the 1983 academic year, students from eighty-six countries came to study in Athens.

Radio was the first technology that Ohio University explored to carry educational programming. More than thirty years ago, service was initiated on an FM station with limited power. Carrier-current program experiments preceded FM broadcasting. Today, the university operates separately programmed AM and FM stations, principally for public service purposes. Broadcast television operations, which began twenty years ago, have expanded to use two transmitters and two translators linked by a microwave interconnection system. These stations provide a typical mix of instructional programs for elementary and secondary school youngsters and adult students, locally originated information and cultural programs, and programs acquired through national, state, and regional networks.

Growth of on-campus uses of television has kept pace in Athens with broadcast services. Today, 85 percent of the academic departments on campus use closed-circuit instructional television services. Applications include direct instruction, course enrichment, and self-evaluation in the classroom. Instructional experiences are provided through a closed-circuit system linking about 100 classrooms around campus with a Media Distribution Center. Small television systems are also used to permit students or faculty members to produce their own material or to play back recordings on cassette or reel-to-reel videotape machines. Many departments own some equipment.

Cable television programming was initiated on Channel 7 of the Athens Community Antenna Television (CATV) system three years ago. This new service includes about twelve hours a day of locally produced or acquired programming, which is unique in the area. While the broadcast television services are accessible throughout the region, the cable channel is a strictly local venture providing public service and continuing education programs.

The most recent technological application of radio and television is the direct, two-way, interactive microwave television teaching link that opened in January 1983 to share faculty resources between the university's Athens and Lancaster campuses. A growing range of courses, conferences, and special programs is making use of this new technology.

All the services just mentioned are managed through a single administrative unit, the Telecommunications Center. Of course, there are other media resources available to the university community. Computer and audiovisual services, including work stations for computer-assisted instruction, are provided through a single administrative unit, the Computing and Learning Services Department, which also manages the university's telephone system. The other major administrative unit that manages regular technological systems for learning is the library. There, as in most modern libraries, computer systems provide access to bibliographic files and search indexes.

One other piece of background needs to be provided. The College of Communication at Ohio University is its largest professional degree-granting college. More than 2,200 majors study journalism, interpersonal communication, telecommunications and broadcasting, visual communications, and communications management. A major goal for the university has been to provide these students with opportunies for laboratory experience. This experience is provided primarily through work in the Telecommunications Center, where about 320 students are involved each year.

In summary, the key elements that have shaped the university's approach to telecommunications applications are its rural setting; its comparatively small population base, which has led to the development of independent study services; plus the strong position of related communication programs and the need to provide laboratory opportunities for students who, in a metropolitan area, might find them at commercial broadcasting stations. Its view of these services is shaped by the tradition of a land-grant institution. Because it views its future as closely tied to its principal service area, its programs reflect concerns shared by the university and the broad community. Without rejecting local responsibilities, the university has extended its resources as a member of the international community, and it uses some of the tools of telecommunications to do this new job.

I will use our experience to illustrate how one institution has realized or is striving to realize each of the educational objectives stated earlier. As Bernard J. Luskin, president of Coastline Community College and national leader in the production and use of television course materials for adults, remarked a few years ago, institutions involved in the application of technical systems to higher education goals are still in the cottage industry stage. We have, he said, a great deal to learn from each other. While the organizational structure for sharing these materials nationally has improved since that time, as well as the quality of the resources available, his point still holds. The stories that follow are offered in the hope that some of the elements of our experience will be useful to others working in the same cottage industry.

Realizing Educational Objectives: A Case Study

Time and Place Flexibility for Nontraditional Students. The use of technologies to address the special needs of adult students is part of a major commitment by Ohio University to lifelong learning. While our focus in this chapter is on telecommunications, use of audio and video technologies must be seen as part of a broad set of support services for adults. These services include evening and weekend courses, computer-based career counseling, individual program planning, experiential learning assessment, and correspondence study options. Coordination and focus are provided by the Lifelong Learning Office and the Adult Learning Services Office, but responsibility for program development and support is systemwide.

A clear decision was made to incorporate these services into the academic structure of an established residential university. Academic review of nontraditional programs and decisions regarding the award of credit follow much the same procedures as those for traditional courses. The system thus vests responsibility for evaluation and accreditation in the hands of interested faculty regardless of the medium of instruction.

Ohio University's most visible application of technology to further time and space flexibility has been the presentation of telecourses over its two television stations. These are program series with accompanying print material and procedures that permit the award of academic credit. Telecourses and telecourse enrollments continue to be seen as the litmus test of the successful application of television to adult instruction. Far from falling out of favor with teachers or learners or being threatened by competing systems, program series with the didactic intent of teaching remain a part of the broadcast schedules of most public educational stations. In the 1983–84 academic year, Ohio University will broadcast twelve such series. The concept of the televised class, which allows the impact of a compelling teacher to be transmitted to people throughout the community, is an old one in educational broadcasting, and it remains at the center of much that we see—or hope to see—on television. Often coupled with other well-designed learning system components, television programs increasingly do what they do best—present new experiences, demonstrations, and the direct impressions of a nonlinear imaging medium.

Cable television is often cited as an ideal medium for telecourse delivery. It has several advantages. It can provide more than one channel of instructional programming, its technical costs are comparatively low, and its need for program material often allows an individual series to be shown several times. Although Ohio University operates a cable television channel in Athens, most of the university's telecourse projects have not used that channel. The reason is that, unlike the broadcast channels, the cable channel reaches people only in one small city, not those throughout the broad region. If the university were operating in an area where the span of cable matched the location of all potential adult learners, cable television would be the desirable distribution instrument, as it already is for urban institutions that have access to metropolitan cable systems. In those locations, the problem is often one of access. The basic allocation of channels for cable service is determined through each community's franchising process. Some universities have recognized the potential uses of cable and taken the necessary political steps locally to assure long-term access for higher education. In other communities, the potential of cable for transmission of telecourses and data and other university services has been lost, often for fifteen years or more.

Most of the telecourses offered by the university are acquired from national suppliers. The producers of these instructional packages often market them through public networks, where producer and user needs can be brought together. Course materials are frequently developed by an institution in response to particular local needs and abilities, then shared with others to recover costs, to acquire working capital for more production, or to extend academic credit opportunities to students nationwide.

Ohio University's criteria for telecourse selection include both academic and broadcast concerns. First, courses that stand alone and that match the university's market interests tend to be selected. General subjects are covered, but there is no effort to present a basic curriculum only through telecourses. For example, the university chose not to participate in a project requiring a multiyear commitment of large amounts of interdisciplinary course materials to provide a basic curriculum. That service was not consistent with the more selective marketing and accrediting strategy for telecourse development adopted both at Ohio University and at other institutions in the state.

Broadcast criteria include concerns about technical and production quality, but these are frequently met by producers offering material nationwide. Of greater concern is the selection of programs that do not require too narrow a background of the viewer and that have a reasonable potential for general audience use. For example, an advanced mathematics course is not likely to be selected. In contrast, a training course for teachers could present information that was also useful for parents and that was accessible without prior training. It should be recognized that most people will view a telecourse simply to learn from it. Some viewers will write for related guides or books to heighten their learning experience. Fewer will go through the formal processes of registration, interaction with the institution, and testing required to earn academic credit. Such a range of course use is entirely consistent with the continuing education and service roles of universities.

Access to these programs is facilitated for nontraditional students by providing some time flexibility within the broadcast schedule. The typical program is repeated at least once in the broadcast schedule, and as far as possible it is offered at times felt to be most useful for the potential student. Time flexibility is increased by students who record programs at home and by placement of recordings at resource centers to which students have access. It could be argued that mailing videocassettes to the limited number of students enrolled for credit would, in some cases, be more cost-effective than broadcasting the courses. That is a reasonable consideration for subject areas that have limited general audience appeal and for courses in which the number of students enrolled is small. Nevertheless, cost comparisons should be done carefully both for conventional delivery modes like mail service and for transmitted programs. It might prove more expensive to mail cassettes to fifteen people in a service area than it would be to broadcast the same programs.

Ohio University's production of telecourses and related materials takes place on a variety of levels. First, independent study materials have been developed to accompany acquired telecourses or broadcast television series with academic potential. For example, an independent study package developed and administered by the English department was tied to a major Public Broadcasting Service (PBS) series of Shakespeare's plays. The series, which was intended primarily for use by the general audience, also provided adult learners with access to high-quality productions of the plays. Study materials tied to these productions offered a unique learning package for nontraditional students in the region.

Second, audio recordings that augment or extend correspondence material have been produced. Although audio recordings are often overlooked in discussions about the new technologies, they provide a high level of time and place flexibility. Because they are used in a variety of instructional settings, audio resources are available on most campuses. For the nontraditional student, audio recordings permit access to lectures, readings, or recorded discussions. They contribute significantly to the learning process, they are easy to use and cost-effective, and the tape recorders used to play them are in the hands of students at all levels.

Third, Ohio University produces entire telecourses. In recent years, these productions have been promoted by local curricular needs that acquired telecourse materials and local resources for the development of such courses could not meet. One recent series "Coping with Kids," illustrates these productions. A thirteen-program series, "Coping with Kids" was authored by Thomas J. Sweeney of the College of Education, produced by the Telecommunications Center, and broadcast on the university's two television stations. Related study materials were developed by the university's Independent Study Through Correspondence program. The course package was offered for graduate and undergraduate credit through the College of Education; graduate students attended discussion group meetings on the university's campuses.

Some general observations about this telecourse should encourage others interested in similar projects. First, the course materials remain useful today and continue to be a part of the university's telecourse schedule for adult students. Second, although these projects required an initial investment and some risk, a study done in 1981 indicated that use and marketing of this set of course materials over a three-year period had returned about $2 for every $1 invested through related tuition, fee, and residual income. Third, the course, which dealt with early childhood behavior modification, was of high interest to a general audience. The series provided valuable parenting experiences for families in the service area and demonstrated again that properly designed instructional television programs can be accessible to viewers who simply watch because of interest. Enrolled students received academic depth and measured learning through correspondence study and testing, readings, and interaction with others in discussion groups.

Other productions have dealt with the guidance and counseling needs of adult learners. Ohio University has served as a regional center for professionals interested in expanding adult learner programs through the services of the Council for the Advancement of Experiential Learning (CAEL). The university's production capability in television and independent study has led to a series of cooperative projects funded in part by the Kellogg Foundation. Two television series and related study materials were produced for Project Learn Phase I, a CAEL-managed national project to strengthen the ability of local institutions to deliver adult learner support. The first series, "Transitions," illustrated the process of prior learning assessment by showing how individuals used experiential learning options to build their academic programs. The second series, "Making a Living Work," showed the role that education played in adult life transitions. Both series were broadcast with credit-related material offered locally, and both will be used on videocassettes as part of the counseling process at the university's Adult Learning Services center.

Broadcasting operations at Ohio University have required the development of physical facilities adequate to produce effective, high-quality television programs for use locally and for distribution to other stations and institutions. That capacity has been built primarily through the application of federal funds provided since 1962 through what is now the Public Telecommunications Facilities Program in the Department of Commerce. These funds are available to support production, transmission, and operational equipment needs for public radio and for the nation's 299 public television stations, more than 200 of which are licensed to university or public authorities. The result of this grant program has been to increase substantially the ability of these public institutions to engage in effective television production work for learning.

Policy concerns have emerged on two levels as telecourse materials have been broadcast and produced at Ohio University. The first, which affects all public institutions in Ohio and which is similar to concerns in other states, has been raised by the caution that prevails among those who determine subsidy levels for state support of higher education. Although subsidy formulas that cover off-campus instruction, and the use of television or other technologies to improve classroom learning is encouraged, the use of television to extend learning to off-campus sites receives no subsidy support. While public institutions have been encouraged by the Ohio Board of Regents to explore these new technologies, they must rely on student fee income to do so. The result is a mixed message for interested institutions. Telecourses often suffer under this economic model when they are compared with traditional courses, because the latter are supported by both fee and subsidy income.

The second level of policy concern involves issues growing out of program production. In an institution, these issues typically include rights of authorship, property ownership, periodic academic review, adequate production time, up-front compensation, and rights to residual income resulting from sale or rental of the property. Ohio University's history with these issues developed from two directions: policies governing the production of material intended for closed-circuit use on campus (not for broadcast) and policies governing off-campus teaching by faculty, including their role in the development and use of independent study materials.

In regard to the production of closed-circuit instructional television materials, it was assumed that release time would be provided to interested faculty as compensation for their work and as a vehicle for assuring adequate time for production. No additional up-front payment was involved. Faculty retained full rights of authorship to scripts or other literary work supporting the series, but the television materials themselves were the property of the university, since its facilities were used, and faculty were participating under contract (on a release-time basis). Faculty review was assured every three years so that the material would not become dated. Net income from the sale or rental of the television programs was divided between the faculty member, the academic department involved, and the university. The move toward broadcast use and nationwide marketing of the university's instructional programs resulted in changes to some elements of this policy.

Faculty who teach courses through traditional techniques off campus or at any of the university's regional campuses have historically received overload compensation in most cases. Faculty members who prepare materials for independent study through correspondence are compensated up front for that effort through additional payments. They can also earn income in later years through utilization, review, and grading of materials. However, the literary correspondence resources become the property of the university with full rights reserved.

Agreements for broadcast telecourses are negotiated separately, but they tend to incorporate elements of each earlier policy. The university retains ownership of the basic television and correspondence material, but faculty can otherwise use notes and their other literary efforts. Even for faculty on contract, up-front added cash compensation is usually provided. Faculty review of the course material is assured every three years. Net income from the sale or rental of the property owned by the university is shared with the faculty author and usually with the academic department involved. Finally, with major offerings, the pattern of using consultants for authorship is increasing. In these cases, full ownership remains vested in the university and its institutional partners in the project, such as CAEL.

Interinstitutional Cooperation. Ohio University is part of an emerging nationwide system supporting telecommunications applications in higher education. There are gaps in this system, especially in its ability to articulate national policies and to share information, but the network of service providers is growing each year at the national, regional, and local levels. These networks described here have provided direct benefits to the university by making use of the national public television system.

Public television is better equipped today to deliver effective postsecondary education programs than it ever has been in the past. Use of earth satellite systems for program distribution has permitted the program options in each community to expand, and a broad range of postsecondary programs has been included. Perhaps the best known national provider of television course material for adult students is the PBS Adult Learning Service. Based in Washington, the service works through public television stations and with producers and other agencies to present a national schedule of telecourses from which each community can select programs that meet its local needs. The PBS does not produce programs itself. It acquires national rights from producing organizations and licenses those rights to participating colleges, which work with their local public television station and other institutions of higher education in the area to develop a local broadcast schedule. The colleges pay a license fee to the PBS Adult Learning Service, which it shares with the producers and with local stations to support their operating costs.

The virtue of this model is that it encourages local consortium building and cooperation. It is also effective in returning revenue to those who produce in this field and to the broadcaster or educational cable television operator who distributes the programs. It has been successful in many communities. In the 1982–83 academic year, its second year of operation, the Adult Learning Service expected a total national enrollment of 75,000. In some communities, however, the service has increased the frustration of competing colleges and seen friction between academic institutions and the public television station when station staff did not share enthusiasm for the project. In southeastern Ohio, this model has encouraged interinstitutional cooperation. The availability of programs and institutional support services for faculty and administrators has led to cooperative arrangements between Ohio University's regional campus network and two technical colleges. Twelve telecourses will be broadcast during the 1983–84 academic year.

The PBS is not the only agency that markets television course material. Four regional public television networks, some of which antedate the PBS in addressing program needs in this area, offer similar services. Ohio University is a member of the Chicago-based Central Educational Network (CEN), which uses the same domestic satellite interconnection service as the PBS to deliver its program services. The CEN's particular strength is that it works directly with state postsecondary education agencies to assess needs, seek cooperative production funding, and provide instructional support services. The CEN Postsecondary Education Council includes ten state agencies representing 362 institutions of higher education. Where no single state agency exists with telecommunications-related higher education authority, as in Ohio, states can join by forming a statewide consortium.

In Ohio, fifty institutions of higher education, including Ohio University, have joined the Ohio Postsecondary Telecommunications Council (OPSTC). The council, which is managed by the Ohio Educational Broadcasting Network Commission with the cooperation of the Board of Regents, coordinates telecourse use and represents the interests of the state to the CEN. OPSTC reports on telecourse use statewide indicate strong growth, especially among OPSTC members. For the 1981–82 academic year, total state telecourse enrollment grew by 98 percent, and the number of colleges using telecourses grew by 89 percent over the preceding year.

Ohio University has experimented with models for the statewide distribution of its productions. For example, the university has provided "Coping with Kids" and other productions to public television stations in Ohio for broadcast at no cost. Stations are encouraged to use these programs with local higher education institutions to develop credit course offerings. Study guides are sold to these institutions at a nominal fee. The station is asked to promote the independent study credit option available through Ohio University for individuals who cannot attend meetings of the local class and to promote all available credit options for the course, including the one through Ohio University.

Interinstitutional cooperation is also promoted in Ohio through the chancellor's Higher Educational Telecommunications Advisory Committee. Representing a variety of institutions and professional backgrounds, the committee advises the chancellor and the Board of Regents on state policy issues. Its recommendations have dealt with the subsidy issue, quality assurance and accreditation, interinstitutional cooperative models, staff and faculty training, and the exchange of information about telecommunications.

Cost Sharing. The efforts of the PBS Adult Learning Service, the CEN, and the OPSTC to acquire programs on behalf of their members all represent cost-sharing plans for telecourse delivery. These group buys permit lower costs than an institution or public television station can negotiate alone.

Original production costs can also be shared. The programs produced by Ohio University and CAEL include production, promotion, and marketing support from both organizations as well as direct funding from the Kellogg Foundation. The foundation has recently confirmed additional support for a national network of institutions serving adult learners, including CAEL and Ohio University, through Project Learn Phase II. The project includes funding for another series of television programs and independent study materials for adult learners. At the same time, the Maryland-based National University Consortium is working on a parallel project with money from the Fund for the Improvement of Postsecondary Education. In order to extend the impact of limited funding, the two projects will now be merged through coproduction of a single television series.

Postproduction costs can also be shared through diversified marketing to institutions or individuals with needs similar to those that led to creation of the programs. For example, "Coping with Kids" was produced primarily as a graduate and undergraduate study opportunity for Ohio university students. Postproduction marketing has led to video distribution through Media Five Channel service from the Appalachian Community Service Network, film distribution via the library of the Association for Counseling and Development (formerly the American Personnel and Guidance Association), and distribution on state and regional public television networks.

Preproduction marketing might be a useful possibility that some major postsecondary program producers could explore. When the producer is well known, it is sometimes possible to aggregate production funding through the advanced sale of distribution rights. This model is being used increasingly by producers of major public television series.

New technical system construction may also provide opportunities for cost sharing. Ohio University recently put into operation a two-way microwave television interconnection system linking its Lancaster campus with the main campus in Athens about fifty miles away. The system is primarily intended for direct, live interactive television teaching. However, it can also carry twelve channels of voice or data service between campuses, replacing costly telephone circuits. The cost recovery plan for this system recognizes the money-saving benefits offered by integrating these media.

Recruiting and Public Information. Adult learning programs and the public broadcasting activities of universities permit an institution to contact many potential students whom it might not otherwise reach. Ohio University reaches more people on a regular basis through its broadcasting activities, including the broadcasting of telecourses, than through any other program. In general terms, these people come to know the university through their contact with the stations. An institution should keep the public information value of such outreach programs in mind when it assesses its activities in telecommunications.

While an effort has been made to avoid programs that are institutionally egocentric, occasional special broadcasts directly promote university courses. One such program planned for fall 1983 is designed to promote interinstitutional cooperation by including participants from several area colleges who will outline and answer viewers' questions about the adult learning services available at their institution.

Operation of a cable television channel in Athens has permitted the university to develop graphic listings of community and university events that incorporate much of the information that its public radio stations handle. An extension of that idea may permit experimentation with communitywide listings of available classes and "closeouts" during registration periods. However, the real potential for visually displayed information about course offerings will have to wait until consumer systems are more broadly available for teletext or videotext data services. In the United States, which lags far behind European countries, Japan, and Canada in the development of such services, the Federal Communications Commission has only recently authorized broadcast teletext services by television stations and made similar decisions regarding the use of a portion of radio signals for graphic data transmission.

Teletext is a system that transmits data together with a broadcast television picture, which is displayed on the picture tube when selected by the viewer. Typical teletext operations provide comparatively simple messages and small amounts of data of interest to a rather broad client group. Videotext is a system for accessing large amounts of computer-stored data and displaying them on a television receiver. The process involves telephone interconnection with the computer, and it permits detailed, branching information resources that provide high volumes of data to be used intensively by comparatively few clients.

Both systems may one day provide user-controlled access to information about the course offerings of colleges and universities. For example, in a metropolitan area, all continuing education course offerings for each college could be cross-referenced and placed in a computer for later display via teletext. Avoiding the usual delays of print media, these data could be instantly updated as courses were added or changed. The user could then access that information to learn more about courses of particular interest.

Ohio has taken a major step forward in the exploration of teletext and videotext services. Through a federally funded project managed by the Telecommunications Center at Ohio University, the state has studied information service needs and information dissemination practices of several public agencies and their suitability for teletext and videotext services. It is hoped that this project will lead to a realistic plan for capital equipment and operating support for a full statewide consumer data service via videotext and teletext.

Networking. All the services just described are available because of a flexible, low-cost technical network that permits programs to be shared in Ohio, throughout the nation, and even internationally. That network has been built over the years in response to varying but mutually supportive public goals. The network first included the university's broadcasting stations, which permitted simultaneous reception of learning materials at multiple points throughout the region. That system was then linked by a two-way microwave network through a switching center operated by the Ohio Educational Broadcasting (OEB) Network Commission to all other public television stations in Ohio. The OEB link now provides additional audio and data transmission services, including an experimental project to tie together computers managed by the Ohio Department of Administrative Services. Using this system, the university can cover most of the ground necessary to get to a transmitting station from which signals can be sent to a domestic earth satellite. The cost of satellite distribution is comparatively low, since it is not distance-sensitive. It costs no more to transmit a program from Ohio to Alaska than it does to distribute the same program to a neighboring state. Finally, receiving facilities for audio and video programming are available at the university through its participation in satellite networks operated by the PBS and National Public Radio.

Use of this system for higher education programs can be illustrated by a teleconference produced in Athens in May 1982 in cooperation with CAEL. The teleconference, a live three-hour event about new directions for adult learning involving a distinguished panel of guests, a moderator, and some videotaped material, included one hour of panel discussion, a one-hour break to permit viewers to discuss the issues raised, and one hour of live interaction during which viewers from around the country asked questions of the panel via telephone. This teleconference was the central component in a series of simultaneous regional CAEL meetings at eleven sites across the country. Technically, the program originated in Athens, from which it was sent to the public television station in Toledo using the OEB state network. From there it was carried through rented telephone company circuits to Detroit, the nearest point that could transmit the signal to the domestic earth satellite used by the public television system. The cost of getting the program from Toledo to Detroit, a few miles, was greater than the cost of distributing it nationally by satellite to reception points as far distant as Alaska and Washington, D.C. Once the program had been transmitted back to earth, it could be received by any PBS station. Conference arrangements at each receiving site were made involving those stations through a conference office at the PBS. While telephone questions from the sites were handled by the telephone company, they no doubt also made use of earth satellites.

Future uses of similar networks will be still more flexible and cost-effective. The ground components of the domestic satellite system are changing rapidly. Receivers are proliferating at business sites as providers of data, and audio and visual services have shifted from older terrestrial networks to space technology. Sites for the transmission of signals to satellites are also increasing. Three such facilities are now planned for Ohio. Columbus and New York City both are developing plans for "teleports"—clusters of transmitting equipment to serve public and private clients. Finally, these systems provide easy access to the international community. In the future, Ohio University may use such systems to carry on regular teleconferences with its partners at Mara Institute of Technology in Malaysia.

Sharing Limited Human Resources. Instructional mediation in any form extends intellectual and experiential resources. Human potential is multiplied through television, audio recordings, or computer-assisted instruction, just as it is through books. In the broadest sense, that is the role of telecommunications in higher education and the end result of all of the projects described here.

A clear example of the extension of limited teaching resources can be found in a new project based on the two-way microwave interconnection system linking the university's Athens and Lancaster campuses. This project is seen as a possible model for a broad system linking all campuses of the university and perhaps all public colleges in the region. In January 1983, teaching service was initiated using this intercampus link. Students met simultaneously in Athens and in Lancaster to be engaged in a live, interactive teaching presentation by economics professor Richard K. Vedder. Television cameras and microphones in a studio classroom in each location allowed students and professors to see and hear one another. Vedder presented lectures from both facilities, shifting to Lancaster to test the system and to meet the students there. Other uses of this system have included a mathematics course taught during the following term by Samuel J. Jasper, a library staff training presentation, a continuing education course in international affairs, student counseling for college placement, and an engineering refresher course that included adult students.

As already mentioned, this system will also be used to provide data and audio transmission between campuses. Cost savings from these services will be added to savings in faculty driving time. Low enrollments at one campus can be coupled with enrollments at another location to permit a wider range of course offerings with the same faculty support. Excitement over the potential of this new system has reached faculty in many departments. The College of Arts and Sciences has developed its own committee on educational telecommunications. Competing proposals for system use have multiplied. The interest is apparently due to the faculty-controlled interactive nature of the system and to the relatively casual approach to the design of presentations that it permits.

Student Laboratory Opportunities. The Telecommunications Center model is perhaps the most effective media service at Ohio University in providing opportunities for interested students. One of the largest and best developed programs of this kind in the country, the Center is staff supervised but student operated. That is, students under staff direction provide much of the creative energy on which the Center's services are based. Students work in virtually all sectors of Center operations. This is possible to a large extent because of the university's strong academic programs in telecommunications, journalism, and related fields. These programs attract good students, who come in part because of the chance to work at the center.

This is not to say that these relationships are without tensions. The missions of the academic programs and the Center—a service unit for the whole university—are necessarily different, although they overlap and support each other. Nonetheless, it is possible to develop working arrangements that acknowledge each set of responsibilities. One such arrangement involves management of the university's cable television service. Management of Channel 7 in Athens, including programming, promotion, and operating and technical support, is provided by the Center. This arrangement makes use of the Center's existing management structure and permits a focus on the special needs of the cable audience. Nevertheless, the largest amount of local program production for the service is carried out by a production unit from the School of Telecommunications. Student opportunities for increased production are extended under faculty supervision using this model.

However they accomplish it, it is increasingly important for institutions of higher education to play a strong role in training future professionals for the information industries. For example, the people who will shape future applications of videotext services should learn about the social and cultural context in which they are to operate. The practical facilities of universities offer a range of laboratory opportunities to support that teaching role.

Conclusion

Despite the range of experiences described in this chapter, Ohio University is only now coming to realize much of the potential held by telecommunications systems to support its role in society. Rapid technological change will present opportunities that are difficult to see today. There is a heightened sense of concern about how we manage the changes that the institution can control.

Two general observations are apparent from recent work. First, institutions will work increasingly with systems that permit the integration of instructional media. The television production skills at the Telecommunications Center are now being used to produce recorded dramatizations that illustrate concepts essential to experiencing English as a second language. They are integrated into a computer-assisted instructional program designed by Marmo Soemarmo of the linguistics department. The final format for student use may be videodisks, a medium that permits random access to television material driven by the computer program. System integration is also apparent in use of the two-way interactive television microwave system, which can interconnect computers on all campuses of the university. The FM radio station can now be seen as a possible vehicle for transmitting data, separate from its general audience programming, to update information stored in computers throughout the region. Deregulation of the telephone industry has opened possibilities for university-operated voice channel services that use some of these same facilities. The explosion in the application of domestic earth satellites for communication extends those possibilities internationally.

Second, if we are confronted with the need to plan for an increasingly complex technological environment, do we have the people required? Can they be trained? Is the institution organized for such a task? Efforts have been made at Ohio University to improve the coordination of planning and management for these purposes, to provide the widest possible range of service options in the future. Our hope is that telecommunications systems will continue to be applied effectively to the broadening of human potential among individuals who are part of the university community. Our job is to be sure that those options for future services are not foreclosed by lack of vision today.

Joseph Welling is director of the Telecommunications Center at Ohio University in Athens, a center that provides public services, instructional programs, and student training opportunities, and is a member of both the board of directors of the Public Broadcasting Service and of its executive committee. He was elected to the board of directors of National Public Radio shortly after its founding in 1970 and served for six years, two as its chairman.

Institutional leaders must address a host of planning, budgeting, training, organizational, and policy issues as they confront the explosion in use of computers on college campuses.

How Computers Are Transforming Higher Education

Robert G. Gillespie

When some of the designers of the early vacuum tube computers discussed the world market for computers in the early 1950s, they estimated that 100 computers of the class of IBM 704 would be needed at most. Today, the computational speed and memory of the average personal computer exceed the capability of those systems, and it has been forecast that more than 3 million systems will be sold in 1983. The number of computers far exceeds 10 million when we consider the number of microprocessor chips built into cars, instruments, airplanes, washing machines, and ovens.

Clearly, the computer has moved into the mass age; it is as if we have moved from making our own shoes to buying them from a shoe factory. The use of computers is no longer limited by the scarcity of software or by the need for users to have special training or to fashion specialized programs. Instead, microcomputer magazines are filled with advertisements for user-friendly software and hardware designed for a variety of activities ranging from entertainment to accounting and instruction.

It is not surprising, then, that colleges and universities are in the midst of grappling with the issues surrounding the explosion in the use of computers on campus. The original uses of computers—to solve scientific and administrative problems too large or too time-consuming to handle any other way—are now just a small part of the picture. Faculty in every discipline are realiz-

P. J. Tate, M. Kressel (Eds.). *The Expanding Role of Telecommunications in Higher Education.*
New Directions for Higher Education, no. 44. San Francisco: Jossey-Bass, December 1983.

ing the potential of the personal computer for word processing, accessing data for research, and communicating with colleagues by electronic mail. Increasing numbers of students are beginning to use computers before entering college; in fact, learning to use a computer keyboard is becoming as normal for students as learning to drive a car already is. Thus, higher education institutions, whether they develop coherent strategies for computing on campus or not, will be transformed by both faculty and student demand for computer access.

Twenty years ago, the role of computing in higher education was examined in a series of reports aimed at determining the value of computers to education, the approaches that the federal government should follow, and the funds that would be required. The so-called Rosser report (Committee on Uses of Computers, 1966), which was commissioned in 1962 by the National Research Council, identified the needs of scientific research for computers and the steps needed to increase the capabilities of universities for use of computers. The report recommended doubling the amount of computing in higher education between 1964 and 1968 by doubling the federal share of campus computing budgets. The report pointed out that the opportunity for gain in national capabilities far exceeded the amounts to be invested.

In 1967, the so-called Pierce report (President's Science Advisory Committee, 1967) took a more general perspective on computing in higher education. Tracking the early developments in time-sharing and anticipating the surprising breadth of applications, the report reinforced the belief that computers were important in all education, not just in the sciences and engineering. It provided a simple measure for undergraduate cost per student for academic computing: $60 a year. This measure was based on an average use of 17.25 hours per year. Note that the estimate did not include either administrative or research use. Moreover, the report emphasized the need for interactive computing. Computing was viewed as a laboratory activity in which interaction was a key to effective learning. Finally, the report stressed that, to remedy the deficiency in undergraduate computing, the federal share should be increased so that the total sum spent on instructional computing should reach $414 million by 1972.

Unfortunately, neither report led to any significant total increase in the federal investment in computing. While programs for institutional approaches to computing and networks were supported by the National Science Foundation, the amount of federal funds spent has remained approximately constant since 1964 at $80 million per year. Figures 1 and 2 show that the total amount of funds spent on computing in higher education grew rapidly between 1965 and 1981 and that the distribution of expenditures changed, with a significantly larger percentage going to administrative use.

While computing expenditures have been growing, they have not kept pace with the demand for computing services. As recently as 1981, the amount spent by higher education for computing was only about 2 percent of the total funds spent by higher education in that year. Thus, conflicts over scarce com-

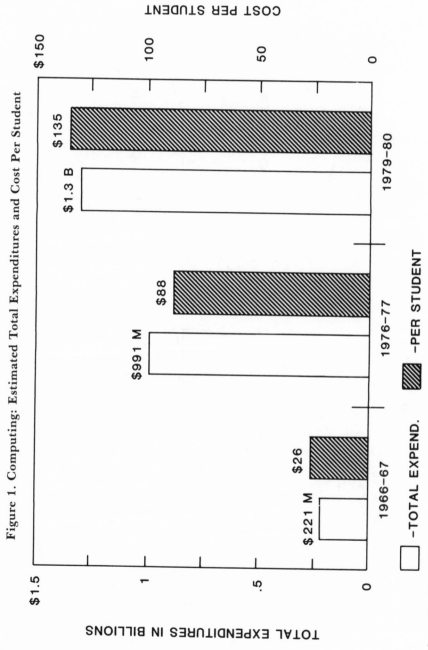

Figure 1. Computing: Estimated Total Expenditures and Cost Per Student

COST PER STUDENT

$150   100   50   0

TOTAL EXPENDITURES IN BILLIONS

$1.5   1   .5   0

$135
$1.3 B
1979-80

$88
$991 M
1976-77

$26
$221 M
1966-67

☐ –TOTAL EXPEND.   ▨ –PER STUDENT

Source: Hamblen, 1981.

Figure 2. Distribution of Expenditures

1969-1970
$473 M

ADMINISTRATION
34%

RESEARCH
32%

INSTRUCTION
30%

OTHER
4%

1980-81
$1.3 B

ADMINISTRATION
50%

RESEARCH
20%

INSTRUCTION
25%

OTHER
5%

Source: Hamblen, 1981.

puting resources are becoming increasingly common, particularly in the climate of general cutbacks in higher education. In the competition for these resources, there is a danger that instructional and research needs may be slighted in favor of administrative needs. For example, if the bursar's office feels that new computing equipment is needed in order to process the payroll efficiently, few presidents will turn down the request, especially if it is presented by a vice-president for administration or finance to whom the computer center reports. In contrast, an academic department's appeal for extensive computer time to tap a national research data base may be viewed as an unjustifiable luxury.

The trend toward ownership of personal computers by students, faculty, and administrators complicates the issue of developing a coherent strategy for computing on college and university campuses. A few institutions, including Carnegie-Mellon, Stevens, Drexel, and Clarkson, already either require or provide personal computers for every student. This change in the types of computers on campus and in who pays for them represents a change in the character of computing as well. The functions of existing computer centers are rapidly evolving from computation to communications, networks access, and data base management activities. The emphasis is shifting from calculation and computation to information processing. In other words, the question is not, How can I use this computer center? but, How can I use this tool? This shift to the view of the computer as a universal tool in higher education is not surprising when we consider that education is concerned with the acquisition and manipulation of information. Moreover, the power of the computer lies in its ability to manipulate abstract symbols rapidly. Finally, the rapid drop in the cost of producing computers is leading to applications in areas that were not considered cost-effective five years ago. Today, a personal computer can provide text-editing and printing capabilities for less than $2,000. Since prices are expected to decline even more, an administrator or faculty member has a strong incentive to invest in this tool, rather than in, say, a new typewriter or a new car.

However, in order for faculty, students, and administrators to benefit fully from the new options that personal computers create, new investments in facilities and services are required. The benefits of owning one's own computer are limited, for example, if one lacks a mechanism for moving information to other computers or for using information stored in other computers. To send a message to someone on campus via computer, for example, requires an orderly development of electronic mail services. And, in order to use the library's computerized bibliographic services, appropriate software must exist along with a campus communications network. This means that standards to enable individual users to cope with the babble of computer dialects and communications protocols are needed. In short, all potential computer users must be taken into account, and an orderly process of development must be put into place. The remainder of this chapter discusses some of the steps in that process, focusing on the issues and questions that must be addressed.

College and university administrators need to address four general areas — planning, budgeting, strategies for transition, and organizational and policy issues — and in each area they need to answer several key questions.

Planning

There are three key questions in the area of planning. First, who will do the planning for integration or sharing of computing and communications services — ad hoc faculty committees, consultants, or deans' task forces? Second, how will this planning fit into existing university planning processes? Third, how will personal computers on campus be linked to the campus communication system?

Just as the organization of computing services varies widely at individual colleges and universities, each campus will have a different approach, definition, and strategy for planning. Some campuses already have a committee charged with writing a campus plan and building a consensus for the goals that it states. Other campuses will locate their planning efforts within budget and allocation processes, and still others will assume that planning can only be done by the schools and departments.

However a consensus on campus information service issues is achieved, it will be needed. Although computer users on campus today may see a need for increasing the access to computing services — and thereby the investment in computing services — others may resist these changes, contending that too much emphasis is being placed on technology at the expense of other campus priorities. Consider working backward from 1988 — what steps and investments will be needed to meet increasing service demands by computer users? The need for long-range planning for investments in computing services can best be illustrated by comparing expenditures for libraries with expenditures for instructional computing. Each year, the national expenditure per student for libraries is around $100, while the expenditure per student for instructional computing is less than $30. Think of the implications for campus budgeting if a campus decided to follow the example of colleges that provide a microcomputer for every student — especially if the price for a useful communication and word processing system drops from the current $1,500 to $2,000 figure to $500 within the next five years. Setting those goals now would be the crucial first step so that allocation of scarce campus resources — or necessary fund raising — could follow.

Van Horn (1980, pp. 13-14) suggests four viewpoints that could be considered in setting university goals: "Elective computing could be viewed as an interesting subject which students may study if they wish. Literacy computing is a basic area of knowledge, and every student should understand its essential features. Skill computing is viewed as an intellectual skill similar to natural languages and mathematics. Foundation computing is viewed as the key technology for information processing, and information processing is viewed as the fundamental process in learning." Planning could start by identifying the relevance of computing to individual university goals and objectives. This step is critical to the development of any plan or planning approach, since it represents the university strategy at a goals level.

Budgeting and Allocation of Resources

In this area, there are six key questions. First, how should scarce computing resources be allocated — arbitrarily, historically, through cost centers? Second, who should set priorities for computing budgets? Should investments be made in the departments or offices that currently use information services, or should they be devoted to stimulating new uses? Third, to what extent will faculty, students, and administrators need to share in the costs of new information services? Fourth, what metric should be used for planning for instruction and research access — terminal hours, central processing unit (CPU) hours, dollars, number of students per terminal, cost per student? Fifth, what are the budgetary implications of the space requirements of new computing equipment and its support requirements? Sixth, how will new computing services be funded?

The special problems raised by allocation of computing services can be illustrated by comparing it with library resource allocation. In the library, allocation mechanisms are in place to allow the distribution of services to competing faculty and students. For example, the allocation of the book-purchasing budget is handled differently from the allocation of books to users. Luckily, no one is allowed to back a semitrailer up to the library steps and pack in a whole book collection. Unfortunately, the computing service issue has that problem, since a relatively small number of users can dominate any service use.

The allocation of computing facilities is also analogous to the allocation of laboratory facilities. It is clear that classes and research must involve scheduling use of laboratories and costly instruments. Since one can see how busy a facility is by counting the lab sites occupied, planning and allocation are clearly tied to the normal planning process for class scheduling. However, computer use, especially when it is shared among a large number of users, is far more difficult to measure. For example, a minicomputer may be able to support sixty users when they form a homogeneous group, as in a class teaching introductory programming, but it could be brought to its knees (that is, the response time to a command sent from a terminal might lengthen from less than one second to as long as a minute) if just a few students ran statistical data.

One issue that complicates allocation is charging for services. If federal grants and contracts represent a use of shared computer facilities, then federal rules for cost allocation prescribe limits. One important consequence of the federal rules is that all users must pay for the use. You cannot give away use without also giving it away to the federal government.

Typically, the estimated cost of running the computer facility is used to derive a rate for service use. The university contribution tends to be fixed because of annual or biennial budgeting. The university's share of use is allocated by allocating a share of the dollars identified for the budget. That is, each dean receives a dollar budget that represents a share of all services (central processing unit, terminals, memory, consulting, and so forth). However, the charges are usually only on the computer uses.

The dean usually cannot take the allocated funds and spend them on other services — for instance, on laboratory equipment. Thus, the allocation is described as "green stamps" or "funny money." These allocation schemes create substantial problems when the services change. Shifting computing services from monolithic and centralized activities to highly decentralized processes can generate substantial obstacles to change. For instance, a dean may feel that a laboratory of microcomputers is more effective educationally than terminal use of central facilities. But, if the only item in the computing budget is allocation of central services, those services cannot be traded for microcomputers. Decentralization of service options requires changes in budgeting processes. But, the decentralization of budgeting still requires addressing three central issues. First, how can very expensive facilities, such as large mass memories, sophisticated graphic equipment, and campus networks be shared to reduce costs? Second, how are the budget levels for services justified? Third, how are demand and supply issues addressed?

Allocation of computing funds can be seen as a highly centralized activity driven from the top down, or it can be viewed as a very decentralized process with competition for resources at the departmental level. Since computing first appeared on campus as a strongly centralized activity, it has tended to be allocated as a top-down process. For example, the budget for computing was often developed as a single budget element, not as separate computing budgets for each educational unit. The second approach has the advantage of requiring the school or dean to weigh the educational value of fulfilling computing needs against other alternatives, such as more faculty or more travel. However, the disadvantage is that resource sharing or effectiveness of computing services can be lessened. Of course, this eventuality must be weighed against the institution's educational objectives.

However, as computing resources have become more varied and as individuals have become more able to determine and satisfy their own computing resource needs, the allocation process has started to change. Since the cost of hardware is steadily declining in comparison to the cost of people, it can be expected that central functions will change from computing and mainframes to information service support and resource sharing for facilities that are too costly to acquire individually. To capitalize on decentralization, the allocation process will have to become more bottom-up and more open to individual initiative.

There is little agreement on the definitions of supply and demand for information services. Since computers were originally very expensive, planning in universities tended to focus on central services and on computer centers. Now, planning requires analysis of educational needs and options. One of the critical allocation issues is what measure should be used to link computing needs and services with the academic needs and services expressed in an academic plan. Since academic planning often centers on the class schedule, methods of planning that link computing plans with the institution's normal budgeting and planning approach will be necessary.

One approach used for allocation, particularly at the undergraduate level, is to use terminal or work station hours as a service metric. Basically, if computing is seen as a laboratory activity, then the amount of time that a student spends using the facilities provides a good measure. Thus, computing the number of hours that a student spends at a terminal or at a microcomputer corresponds to the number of hours that a student spends at a laboratory bench. From this simple measure, estimates for space, cost, and so forth can also be derived. The use of simple models, such as terminal hours per student, can help to define needs in the traditional pattern of courses, students, and disciplines. Of course, specialized services, such as graphics facilities, special software, and data bases, must be identified, and the simple model is not sufficient for these estimates. Also, graduate student use and word processing distort this model. For example, a single graduate student with a Monte Carlo simulation can chew up hundreds of hours (any many hundreds of dollars) of computer time.

Planning for major administrative activities is different from planning for academic needs. Administrative needs, such as accounting, payroll, and institutional research, are driven by the processes proposed. Since most activities involve common data bases, planning involves a relatively small number of participants, in contrast to academic computing. This means that no single computing service will be sufficient. These considerations underline the need for innovative and flexible approaches to the messy business of incorporating information processing needs into the traditional planning and budgeting cycles.

Effective Strategies for Transition

In this area, three questions need to be asked. First, what campus efforts (if any) will be needed for faculty training? Second, what pilot projects or experiments should be initiated? Third, what models for change exist at other institutions?

One of the biggest strategic mistakes that an institution can make is to deal with technological change as if the purchase of hardware were the major problem. Bork (1981) discusses the factors that inhibited rapid introduction of computer-aided instruction. In addition to the hardware costs, several secondary factors retarded the widespread use of such systems: lack of curriculum material, lack of faculty time for curriculum development, the high cost of facilities, the many hours of effort needed to develop quality material, and the teams of specialists needed to develop the material.

With the rapid introduction of personal computers on campus and the mass production of software, new problems are emerging for technology innovators. For example, for years conventional wisdom about computers stressed the role of economy of scale as the key to cost-effectiveness. But, mass production of microcomputers and software has made the cost per byte of storage on small systems cheaper than it is on many large systems. Therefore, planning for technological change requires new strategies, such as developing, supporting, and identifying good software and developing the framework of support (networks, software, and so forth) needed to enhance personal computer productivity.

One effective way of introducing any new technology is to ensure that there are many experiments, so that successes can be quickly replicated. As already noted, some private institutions have decided to require all entering students to purchase a personal computer; support services will then be expanded to meet user demand. Another ambitious experiment is the joint effort between IBM and Carnegie-Mellon, in which the university will provide not only the entire support system needed for all faculty and students to use personal computers but the computers themselves. Public institutions, which have less flexibility in establishing new fees or in increasing tuition costs, are choosing less visible and less large-scale strategies for transition. For example, at the University of Wisconsin–Madison a showroom of personal computers and support staff are available to help users to make decisions about the purchase of hardware and software. A number of schools have arranged with hardware vendors to provide discounts to faculty and students who wish to purchase microcomputers.

Since one of the most powerful resources at the university is the human resources—students, faculty, and staff—all potential users should be involved in transition pilot projects. For example, the dean of engineering at Stanford provided microcomputers to faculty members who were committed to learning to use them. Some universities have loaned computers to departments for experimental use in instruction. Administrative use of personal computers can also be stimulated by loan programs, since the goal at this stage is to get as many people as possible to learn how to use this new tool. Other steps that the transition can take include establishing ad hoc and visiting committees to study computing organizations; interesting academic administrators in sessions dealing with computing issues at annual meetings of the American Association for Higher Education, the National Association of State Universities and Land-Grant Colleges, the Association of American Universities, and so forth; attending seminars on planning for computing in higher education arranged by EDUCOM, a nonprofit consortium aimed at stimulating resource sharing with regard to computing; promoting activities by groups previously uninterested in computing issues, such as faculty senates; and placing such issues as computer literacy or software copyright on the agenda for regents and trustees.

Organizational and Policy Issues

Each campus will eventually have to tackle a number of organizational and policy issues. First, what institutionwide policies already exist, and what policies need to be developed for such issues as security, protection of privacy, and rights of staff and students in software development? What rights to information should exist? Second, what policies already exist, and what policies need to be developed for resource sharing, and how will these policies be related to the decentralization of computing facilities? Should the university consider a policy of cost recovery for computing services? Third, what policy should the institution adopt toward personal computers and their support? How much personal investment will be expected of students, faculty, and staff? Will this policy imply shifts in funding? Will it imply mergers of currently separate information services? Fourth, how will the institution define computer literacy? Should it be expected? Who should tackle the problem — deans, faculty, computer centers? If curriculum development is needed, who will be responsible for it, and what support will be needed? Fifth, how will standards for communication and connection be developed? Sixth, should new organizational entities or structures be established to handle the growth of computing and communications over the next five years?

On most campuses, the growth of information services has led to a situation in which offices report to different vice-presidents and executive officers: The library reports to one person, the academic and administrative computer services to another, communications and printing to another, instructional media to another, and mail and reproduction services to still another. Yet, technology is driving all these information sources together. Realization that all these separate offices are associated with the production and distribution of information on campus is growing. The task of each chief executive officer is to consider the institution's current organizational structure with regard to information services and to initiate a process of developing options that will work both politically and organizationally.

Some institutions have decided that all offices with information services functions will serve on a telecommunications system planning task force. Others are leaving their current organizational structure intact, but they are assigning oversight of the entire system to a single vice-president. Still others are either forming new advisory committees of students, faculty, and staff to explore policy options in such areas as software rights or privacy, or they are using existing campus committees for this purpose. Whatever structure is developed, territorial battles that could slow the development of campus-wide shared information services are inevitable. As new priorities emerge, the separate fiefdoms will decide either to cooperate or to war. This underscores the need for involving many constituencies in the process of identifying the university's information assets and developing policies to manage those assets.

National Computing Issues and Actions

As a variety of studies have indicated (Machlup, 1962; Porat, 1977; Bell, 1973), the United States is changing from a farming and manufacturing society into an information society, in which the value of human capital is critical. Since one of the major functions of higher education is the production of human capital, and since the demand for graduates with information occupation specialities far exceeds the supply, it is becoming increasingly essential for students who enter college in the 1980s to have access to a full range of computing and information services. At most colleges and universities, the computing courses are already swamped, and the number of jobs available to new graduates in computer-related fields reaches ratios ranging from four to one to ten to one (Hamblen, 1981).

Gillespie and Dicaro (1981) identified the opportunities and changes in higher education created by computing, and they explored the role of higher education in helping to maintain this nation's position of technological leadership. They pointed out that a national investment in computing is important, because other nations are developing highly integrated plans for their emerging information economies, plans that could threaten the position of the United States with respect to trade, national security, technological innovation, and productivity.

These authors also identified the key agents in shaping national policies and change strategies with regard to computing: First, of course, are the colleges and universities, represented not only individually but collectively by their professional organizations and associations. Foundations can also play a role as well as all the industries that depend on graduates trained in and familiar with information services and high technology. Congress could take the lead in identifying services and high technology. Congress could take the lead in identifying priorities and resources. The executive branch of the federal government and such federal agencies as the National Science Foundation and the Department of Education could also become involved.

Some national initiatives are already under way. After receiving the study's recommendations from a panel chaired by Irving Shain, chancellor of the University of Wisconsin–Madison, the National Science Foundation (NSF) and the National Science Board (NSB) considered the establishment of a special commission on computing and higher education (Gillespie and Dicaro, 1981). However, since the science education crisis has dominated the attention of the NSF and the NSB, the establishment of a special commission on computing was deferred until the Commission on Precollege Education in Mathematics, Science, and Technology (1982) completed its work.

The shortage of human capital is drawing the attention of a number of industry and trade groups. For example, both the American Electronics Association and the Computer and Business Equipment Manufacturing Association have identified the problem through surveys, and they are moving to develop appropriate strategies. Individual companies are also taking steps to assist colleges and universities in meeting their hardware and software needs for computing education. The venture involving I.B.M. and Carnegie-Mellon mentioned earlier is even broader in that it reaches all students, not just those in computer-related fields.

In addition to the individual activities occurring at colleges and universities, the National Association of State Universities and Land-Grant Colleges has established a committee on education and technology. Currently chaired by Irving Shain, the committee is acting as a central focus for the issues of computing and higher education. Other professional associations, such as the American Association for Higher Education and the Council for the Advancement of Experiential Learning are sponsoring conferences and workshops to explore the impact of the computer revolution.

Finally, congressional hearings have been held to identify some of the problems involved and the opportunities for addressing the issues. The Office of Technology Assessment (1982) has issued a major report, and the issues of computing and higher education were discussed during the hearings on the National Engineering and Scientific Personnel Act of 1983, and recommendations were made for an initiative to accelerate the expansion of access to information services for faculty and students.

Conclusion

Five recommendations, addressed primarily to the chief executive officers of institutions of higher education, can summarize the points raised in this chapter and provide ideas for institutional change with regard to computing and communications:

First, identify campus goals for information services. This is the most important action, since choices about information services, budgets, and strategies all derive from the review and establishment of goals. Van Horn's (1980) computing categories—elective, literacy, skill, and foundation—can be used to stimulate the linking of institutional mission with the function of computing. Goals must also be examined within disciplines and support services areas. Participation by many constituent groups will be an important part of the process of setting goals.

Second, assess the institution's information assets. What are the institution's information assets, not only the equipment but the human resources—faculty, staff, and students? What organizations are involved? What procedures exist? Who is currently responsible for information services? How are resources allocated? Such self-assessment is critical in preparing for any major change. Unfortunately, in the usual assessment, too little attention is paid to any resources but the machines.

Third, develop an investment plan for information services. Use the same care and effort that would go into developing a capital budget to develop a plan that includes services, communications, computers, terminals, support, space, and facilities. What faculty training is necessary? What projects, demonstrations, and incentives will be included in the strategy?

Fourth, review campus policies and allocation and budget procedures for information services. The policies, procedures, and processes will shape the institution's response. The dynamics of the information area are such that technology will quickly outdistance rigid plans. Thus an emphasis on process, strategy, and approach is critical. Processes are embodied in policy and procedures. What will be done about students' software rights? Who will make the allocation decisions? Who will review equipment and software acquisitions for resource-sharing opportunities? How will campus standards be established and audited?

Fifth, identify resource-sharing opportunities. Ideas are the most important resources to be shared. What informal exchanges can be instituted? What organizations are effective in providing an opportunity at a national level—such as EDUCOM or SIGUCC, the special-interest group for university computing centers of the Association for Computing Machinery? What efforts are such national groups as the Association of American Universities and the National Association of State Universities and Land-Grant Colleges stimulating?

In a recent address, Fred Davison (1982, p. 6) president of the University of Georgia, said: "From a curriculum perspective, the compression of time reduces the half-life of certain knowledge bases from decades to years, or, in some high technology fields, from years to months. Textbooks are outdated before they can be published and put into students' hands. Knowledge gained over a period of four to eight years of intensive university study may become obsolete in half that time. Skills painstakingly learned at the laboratory bench can be obviated overnight through the introduction of automated data collection and process control systems."

Davison points out that the traditional focus of higher education has been to teach content, not process. However, introduction of new technologies has caused both the content and the process of instruction to change. Technology has even been a factor in the emergence of new disciplines. Today, the computer may be changing the university in even more fundamental ways than technologies of the past already have. Will the university become simply a machine for the production, storage, and distribution of information, or will it remain an institution that accumulates and passes on the wisdom and knowledge of society? The introduction of computers is certainly the catalyst for a fundamental reexamination—perhaps even a transformation—of the university.

References

Bell, D. *The Coming of Postindustrial Society.* New York: Basic Books, 1973.
Bork, A. *Learning with Computers.* Bedford, Mass.: Digital Press, 1981.

Commission on Precollege Education in Mathematics, Science, and Technology. *Today's Problems: Tomorrow's Crises.* Washington, D.C.: National Science Board, National Science Foundation, 1982.

Committee on Uses of Computers. *Digital Computer Needs in Universities and Colleges.* Publication 1233. Washington, D.C.: National Academy of Sciences, National Research Council, 1966.

Davison, F. "Coping with Technological Change: Technology as a Catalyst for Education." In D. B. Randall (Ed.), *Proceedings of the University Executive Program.* Corvallis: Oregon State University, 1982.

Gillespie, R. G., and Dicaro, D. A. *Computing and Higher Education: An Accidental Revolution.* Seattle: University of Washington, 1981.

Hamblen, J. *Computer Manpower—Supply and Demand by States.* (4th ed.) St. James: Missouri Information Consultants, 1981.

Machlup, F. *The Production and Distribution of Knowledge in the U.S.* Princeton, N.J.: Princeton University Press, 1962.

Office of Technology Assessment, U.S. Congress. *Informational Technology and Its Impact on American Education.* Washington, D.C.: U.S. Government Printing Office, 1982.

Porat, M. U. *The Information Economy.* Washington, D. C.: U.S. Government Printing Office, 1977.

President's Science Advisory Committee. *Computers in Higher Education.* Washington, D.C.: U.S. Government Printing Office, 1967.

Van Horn, R. L. "Academic Computing—How Much is Enough." In D. B. Randall (Ed.), *Proceedings of the Eleventh Annual Seminar for Academic Computing Services.* Corvallis: Oregon State University, 1980.

Robert G. Gillespie is vice-provost for computing and a lecturer
in computer science at the University of Washington. He is coauthor
of a study for the National Science Foundation, Computing and
Higher Education: An Accidental Revolution *(1981).*

The historic concepts of open competition in the delivery of higher education and of strict regulation of telecommunications are undergoing fundamental changes that have enormous consequences for the delivery of educational services.

Telecommunications and Higher Education: In Search of a Public Policy

Michael B. Goldstein

It would be difficult to find two areas of public activity that have more divergent histories of regulation and policy formulation than telecommunications and postsecondary education. Almost from its inception, the former has been considered the proper subject of extensive regulation encompassing access to markets, price, types of service, and even content. The case of postsecondary education has been quite different. To the extent that it has been regulated, regulation has traditionally been limited to assessments of quality and to prescription of minimum standards. The evolution of the relative federal and state roles is even more striking. Since many forms of telecommunications transcend state lines by their very nature, an extensive system of federal regulation has evolved. In contrast, postsecondary education has been viewed as an essentially local phenomenon, with regulatory jurisdiction ordinarily left to the individual states. Indeed, it has become virtually an article of political faith that control of education (as distinguished from its financing) is exclusively a state and local function. The following excerpt from the General Education Provisions Act (1983), the housekeeping statute for federal education programs, illustrates this approach: "No provision of any applicable program shall be construed to authorize any department, agency, officer, or employee

P. J. Tate, M. Kressel (Eds.). *The Expanding Role of Telecommunications in Higher Education.*
New Directions for Higher Education, no. 44. San Francisco: Jossey-Bass, December 1983.

of the United States to exercise any direction, supervision, or control over the curriculum, program of instruction, administration, school, or school system" (20 U.S.C. §1232a).

The public policy behind the extensive regulatory framework of telecommunications is derived from two theories: that telecommunications systems constitute a natural monopoly and that those who utilize the airwaves take advantage of a commonly held resource and therefore exercise a public trust. The natural monopoly theory made perfectly good sense when every private telephone user required a separate pair of wires strung between his or her instrument and a central telephone office. Just as it is logical to have only one gas company and one electric utility serve a given location, so it was reasonable to assume that there should only be one telephone company. But, since such a monopoly would prevent the ordinary competitive market forces from controlling price and service, it was also considered necessary to institute government regulation. Without such regulation, it was argued, telephone and telegraph companies could charge whatever they wanted and provide whatever level of service they desired without regard either for the needs of the public or for actual economic value. Since under our federal system things that do not involve activities crossing state lines remain the province of the states, the regulation of rates and service of intrastate telephone services fell to state public service commissions, while interstate service became a federal responsibility.

The regulation of radio, television, and other forms of wireless communication brought into play a restructuring of relationships between the federal government and the states. Since radio transmissions have no regard for political boundaries, and a local station can interfere with or be interfered with by another station hundreds or even thousands of miles away, federal control of the airwaves was established during the earliest days of radio through the exercise of the constitutional provision granting the national government exclusive dominion over interstate commerce, with a concomitant exclusion of the states from the exercise of most elements of control.

The legislation creating the Federal Radio Commission (later the Federal Communications Commission) called for a competitive process for allocation of the radio frequency spectrum based on the premise that those who are allocated a share of this finite natural resource (a radio channel) should demonstrate that their use will serve the public interest. Quite different and in many respects opposite forces have shaped the regulation of postsecondary education in this country. From the very founding of the nation, education has been considered a primary responsibility of the states. While there is nothing in the Constitution that expressly excludes the national government from exercising its dominion over this area, the Tenth Amendment of the U.S. Constitution, commonly termed the Reserved Powers Clause, has been taken to afford the states preeminence in this area. As the Tenth Amendment states, "The powers not delegated to the United States by the Constitution nor prohibited by it to the states are reserved to the states respectively or to the people." The effect of this early political interpretation has been to preclude the development of the kind of national postsecondary education system that exists in virtually every other country.

Another characteristic of postsecondary education that shaped its regulatory framework is the absence of natural restrictions on competition. Since there are theoretically no limits to the number of purveyors of education services who could serve — or seek to serve — a particular clientele, it can be argued that the traditional forces of competition and the marketplace should be sufficient to assure public access to the best service at the best price. Of course, the fact that regulation is not necessitated by natural phenomena (for example, allocation of scarce spectrum space) does not mean that regulation does not occur. Indeed, ostensibly free market forces can be — and have been — significantly distorted by government intervention.

This intervention has been exercised in several quite different ways. Direct regulation is essentially the exclusive domain of the states, with all but nine states now requiring the licensure of institutions that purport to offer postsecondary instruction. Although the requirements for licensure vary widely from state to state, ranging from the most exhaustive to merely perfunctory examinations of quality and fitness, all requirements are premised on the right of the state to prescribe minimum standards for the delivery of educational services. In contrast to the licensure of telecommunications entities, the stated purpose is not to determine whether one institution is more fit than another to provide the service but whether the institution meets a minimum standard of qualification, which in theory is quite independent of what its competitors provide.

The development of coherent public policy to guide and foster the symbiosis of telecommunications and postsecondary education should be a matter of considerable national interest and concern. Unfortunately, experience indicates that the contrary is the case. In an earlier review of public policy issues affecting the utilization of instructional television for postsecondary education (Goldstein, 1980, p. 41), I wrote that "to a remarkable degree, the federal government has avoided the creation of a coherent and consistent set of policies to guide the development of this field." Today, that statement remains true not only for instructional television but for the entire range of instructionally related telecommunications, including the rapidly expanding use of computers. The same thing is true of regulation and public policy formulation at the state level.

This is not to say that the absence of coherent federal and state policies on telecommunications and postsecondary education implies an absence of federal and state involvement. As already noted, quite the contrary is the case. But, the problem that I described in 1980 is still with us today: Because there is no coherent policy towards the conjunction of telecommunications and postsecondary education, the public policy and regulatory frameworks that do exist operate primarily to serve other purposes. Thus, the constraints and stimuli imposed on this field by government arise largely from forces that are unrelated to the needs and priorities of those who seek educational services or who would otherwise benefit by their provision. Indeed, instead of encouraging and facilitating the use of telecommunications for adult learning as discussed elsewhere in this volume, these policies all too frequently tend to act as constraints and disincentives on such use.

In my earlier analysis (Goldstein, 1980), I identified several areas where public policy or its absence affected the ability of the postsecondary education communicty to exploit the potential of telecommunications. It is useful to reexamine these areas today in light of changing perspectives on the relative roles of the federal government and the states, the new emphasis on the training and retraining of the nation's work force, the need to close the perceived technology gap and increase productivity, and the position of our colleges and universities as the chief providers of postsecondary instruction.

In 1980, seven areas of public policy appeared likely to impinge on telecommunications and higher education in the coming decade:

1. Federal support for postsecondary education would continue to take an ostensibly marketplace approach, with the overwhelming majority of funds distributed in the form of student financial assistance.
2. The freedom of learners to use federal largesse would continue to be circumscribed by requirements that tended to limit eligibility to traditional programs operated by traditional institutions.
3. Direct federal support for postsecondary education other than student aid would be limited to areas in which an identifiable need corresponded to a broad national interest.
4. The continuing deregulation of telecommunications would have the effect of encouraging the growth of alternative telecommunications technologies, which, particularly when coupled with the commercial exploitation of such technologies, would extend the opportunity for instructional uses well beyond present levels.
5. A decreasing federal presence would be counterbalanced by increased state involvement in the approval and support of postsecondary education, including a widening of state jurisdiction over noninstitutional instruction.
6. The availability of relatively low-cost telecommunications-based vehicles to deliver postsecondary instruction over vast areas would stimulate the establishment of entities whose direct service areas would be multistate or national in scope.
7. The establishment of telecommunications-based multistate or national providers of postsecondary education services would trigger a confrontation both between the federal government and the states to determine the locus of ultimate control.

In the discussion that follows, I will examine the degree and manner through which the underlying policies directly or indirectly affect the use of telecommunications for higher education, and I will project the nature of the public policies that are likely to emerge as the nation moves into the information society of the twenty-first century.

The Marketplace Approach to Federal Support

The present legislative framework ensures that the vast bulk of federal support for postsecondary education comes in the form of student financial assistance. While there is now interest in redirecting some of that support away from the free-choice subsidies that have characterized the system since its inception in the mid 1960s, the basic premise of providing students with at least a portion of the resources that they need in order to acquire the postsecondary education that they desire remains unchanged. In the most general terms, the marketplace approach should favor both the adult learner and the use of telecommunications. Flexibility of learning mode, time, and place, which is a *sine qua non* of a system that successfully serves the needs of adults, is characteristic of telecommunications-based instruction. Premising financial support on the needs of learners, not on the requirements of a particular type of deliverer, should therefore enhance the opportunity of learners to select the most appropriate educational vehicle. The same emphasis on supporting the learner should encourage competition among institutions and others who can deliver the appropriate educational services.

While some characteristics of the present marketplace approach of student aid programs are supportive both of the needs of a broad range of learners and of the use of telecommunications-based systems, it is more likely that new assistance programs aimed at meeting an entirely different set of needs will have a more significant impact. Recognition that the technological evolution of American industry requires the continuing education and training of the work force is resulting in the consideration of a new set of government programs to promote and support such education and training. While it is still too early to tell whether these programs will be student-oriented (that is, whether they will provide learners with resources that they can spend on the kind of training and education that they want from the purveyor of their choice), whether they will be distributed through traditional manpower development channels, whether they will be granted to institutions in the form of direct institutional support or whether they will be granted in the form of tax incentives to employees, employers, or both, the enactment of major new legislation appears certain. What is not clear, however, is the degree to which such initiatives will embrace the new technologies of learning. Past manpower programs do not afford a comforting precedent, but the current enthusiasm for the computer may overcome this bias.

For telecommunications-based learning, the marketplace approach appears to be preferable, since as an emerging field its proponents might be at a disadvantage in competing for allocation of resources under an institution-oriented system. Nevertheless, the marketplace approach does not necessarily represent a free market. As I will discuss in the following section, constraints on how learners can spend the resources made available by government can be as limiting as defining the institutional recipients of direct support.

Limitations on Eligibility

Access and choice are laudable goals, but in and of themselves they are meaningless if a particular class of individuals cannot obtain the funds or if the choice of a particular mode of learning or delivery is precluded. Since their inception under the landmark Higher Education Act of 1965, federal student aid programs have been directed towards traditional students (that is, eighteen- to twenty-two-year-olds enrolled full time) who attend traditional colleges and universities where traditional modes of instruction prevail. The drafters of these programs in the Congress and in the executive branch make no apologies for their inclination to target available resources to the customary college-age cohort. The bias against students outside that cohort also extends to delivery systems that differ from the customary. The federal student aid programs are designed around full-time classroom-based resident instruction. While these programs do allow some deviation from this standard, each such deviation necessitates a conceptual reconfiguration of the delivery system into its traditional equivalent. The methods used to achieve such parity vary considerably in their accuracy and equity. All too often, however, they deprive the learner of equal access to a delivery mode better suited to his or her needs.

The most flagrant example of this constraint is found in the administration of the education benefits programs of the Veterans Administration. Here, deviations from rules that prescribe the number of clock hours for which a student must attend classes per week over the course of a semester or quarter can terminate eligibility for assistance. Indeed, the words *attend classes* are used in the strictest sense: Telecourses are permitted only to a limited degree, and computer-based instruction remains a gray area. The student aid programs of the U.S. Department of Education are ambiguous in similar ways. Can a student enrolled in five telecourses be considered full-time? The absence of a definitive answer to this type of question imperils access to and use of alternative technologies.

Not only can the nature of the delivery mode be circumscribed; so can the nature of the provider. American postsecondary education prides itself on its self-regulation: Quality control has historically been the province of voluntary associations of institutions, the accrediting agencies. But, regulation, whether public or private, can have the effect of constraining innovation not only in the form of delivery but in the nature of the provider. The rigors of the accreditation process, which relies heavily on peer review, have not infrequently discouraged otherwise traditional institutions from experimenting with nontraditional forms of instruction. Measures developed for customary pedagogies are not always applicable to alternative delivery systems, particularly those that are technology-based. The size and staffing of the campus library has less relevance for a computer-based "distance-learning" system than it does for resident instruction.

Although the need to achieve and maintain good standing with the accrediting agency or agencies can have a chilling effect on innovation, it must be noted that all the regional accrediting agencies that evaluate entire institutions (as contrasted with the specialized agencies that evaluate particular programs, such as music or law) have taken steps in recent years to reduce impediments to innovation. Whether those steps are sufficient remains to be seen. However, measures of the quality of technology-based instructional systems remain in their infancy, and the bias towards the concept that learning requires a critical level of human interaction remains in force. What that minimum level is, if indeed it exists, has yet to be defined, but the result of this predeliction to the personal student-teacher relationship is an unease with anything that interposes an electronic alternative.

If a traditional institution of higher education has difficulty in resolving the conflicts raised by telecommunications-based instruction for accreditation and quality control, a noninstitutional provider is in an even greater quandary. The self-regulating nature of higher education imposed by voluntary accreditation imbues it with some of the qualities of a guild: The putative provider who is outside the family of traditional institutions may be excluded not because of its program but because it simply has different characteristics. Thus, while there are already large corporate conglomerates that have established postsecondary education services as an integral component of their structure, the existing accreditation machinery is wary of dealing with non-institutional providers of postsecondary education. While the American Council on Education's Program on Noncollegiate-Sponsored Instruction provides credit hour equivalents for military- or business-provided instruction, and while the Council for the Advancement of Experiential Learning has developed methods for converting nontraditional learning into commonly accepted standards, both methods are limited by the need to transform one form of instruction or learning into another. This problem is likely to become even more complex as telecommunications-based learning systems expand. The few noninstitutional providers of postsecondary education that have been afforded recognition by the accreditation community are still a very distinct minority, and they have had to assume institutional coloration in order to meet the requisite standards. Because telecommunication-based instruction does not require an institutional base, the likelihood that noninstitutional providers will become involved in considerable numbers is very real. Whether the accrediting agencies can deal with such entities on an equitable basis remains to be seen.

Coupled with accreditation is the question of state licensure. The problem for providers of telecommunications-based instruction is that it tends to violate the norms on which state approval is most often granted; that is, on the presence of a facility within the state that possesses suitable faculty, library resources, and the like. As noted later in this chapter, the application of state regulation to telecommunications-based instruction poses serious constitutional as well as programmatic concerns.

The relevance of accreditation and state licensure to the issue of student eligibility for financial aid is manifest: The federal laws governing all student aid programs require the provider to be licensed by the state within which it operates and, generally speaking, to have status with an accrediting agency recognized by the U.S. Department of Education. There are exceptions to the second requirement, but they are of limited applicability, and they may be eliminated entirely by the next revision of the Higher Education Act. A provider that cannot receive accreditation status or licensure is one whose students are excluded from participation in federal student aid programs. There is perhaps no greater impediment to the substantial expansion of telecommunications-based learning than the exclusion of learners from the funds needed to obtain that service.

However, the developing interest in programs aimed at improving productivity and at dealing with structural unemployment and underemployment may give rise to altogether different standards of access to federal assistance. It should be obvious that assistance in extending access to postsecondary education to persons whose skills must be upgraded or changed in order to meet the needs of an evolving technological society must be predicated on characteristics of the learner population very different from those of the traditional college-age cohort. Likewise, the need for this population to take advantage of alternative delivery systems, particularly of telecommunications-based systems, in order to overcome problems of access and time is far greater than it is for the typical full-time college student. It therefore appears likely that, as the nation begins to focus on the need to provide a new echelon of postsecondary education, new ways of assessing eligibility for financial assistance will have to evolve.

Direct Federal Support and Emerging Needs

While federal support for student assistance has shown a steady increase since the mid 1960s, direct federal support for institutions has not kept pace. Indeed, a succession of presidents has taken the position that the proper federal role is to ensure equity, access, and choice through a well-designed student aid program and that direct institutional support should be limited to those narrow areas where there is a special need for intervention. Direct institutional support has been defined as support for research and innovation, very limited support for infrastructure development and rehabilitation, and support in such unique areas as sustaining the historically black colleges, supporting new pedagogies like cooperative education, and helping to subsidize the incremental costs of serving poorly prepared students.

What is the likelihood of direct federal support for telecommunications-based instruction aimed at promoting adult learning? In the narrow context of postsecondary education as it is generally defined, the odds of a major new initiative seem very remote, except in regard to computers. Congress seems to be fascinated by computers. In this it has been encouraged mightily by entrepreneurial manufacturers and by visionaries who have replaced the call for a chicken in every pot with a call for a micro in every den, not to mention in every classroom and dormitory suite. Legislation expanding tax benefits for manufacturers who donate computer equipment to schools and colleges was incorporated in the recent tax law revisions, although the more ambitious tax giveaways sought by a few manufacturers were rejected. These off-budget tax benefits are true government subsidies, although they are not reflected in expenditures, and they do not need to be appropriated annually. They represent a strong future trend in federal support for telecommunications-based instruction, particularly insofar as such benefits could be extended to encourage business and industry to establish facilities that allowed their own employees to take advantage of such instructional delivery systems.

Direct federal support is likely to arise from the increasing awareness of the need to retrain the work force and improve its productivity. Congress has been shocked into an awareness of the extent to which technological obsolescence contributes to unemployment and underemployment as well as to the disparities in worker productivity between this nation and such nations as Japan. A great many new programs intended to stimulate instruction in mathematics and the sciences and to encourage the retraining and upgrading of the work force were introduced in the first session of the 98th Congress. While many proposals harked back to old concepts of manpower development, a few looked to the new technologies as affording ways of delivering needed services more economically to a larger clientele.

The likely outcome of these initiatives is the creation of new programs expressly aimed at the adult learner in the context of his or her role as a worker. This work force orientation is likely to bode well for the support of telecommunications-based instructional systems, particularly those that can capitalize on the current enthusiasm for the computer. While some of these programs are likely to be supportive of existing postsecondary institutions, especially the community colleges, which have a well-deserved reputation for their preeminence in the work-related training arena, others may begin to shift resources towards new providers, including businesses and industries that employ or that would employ the worker, as well as new entities created solely for the purpose of retraining the work force. The issues of accreditation, student aid, and even traditional certification may become irrelevant if the federal interest in postsecondary education becomes focused on work force development.

Indeed, the distinction between credit and noncredit learning and with it the emphasis on traditional credentialing may become blurred as the conversion of one form of education into the other becomes more commonplace.

Many of the new programs under consideration use the tax laws as the vehicle for stimulating the delivery of educational services. Some of the ideas now popular include tax breaks for businesses that provide their workers with access to relevant training and education, perhaps in the form of a human capital equivalent to the program of investment tax credits; allocation of a portion of unemployment benefits to education vouchers that can be used for retraining and upgrading; and individual tax funds that individuals can draw on during their lifetime for the education that they need in order to remain competitive in the work force. It seems more than likely that one or more of these approaches will be enacted during the life of the 98th Congress.

Deregulation of Telecommunications and Reregulation of Postsecondary Education

The regulatory winds affecting telecommunications and postsecondary education appear to be blowing in opposite directions. The trend towards reducing the role of government regulation of all forms of telecommunications, from telephone service to direct broadcast satellites is continuing. Increasingly, the Federal Communications Commission takes the position that a service that can be shown to be technically feasible without interfering with another service should be allowed to operate. While the distance between the concept of deregulation and its realization remains significant, and the possibility of ever achieving a totally free-form system remains doubtful for a variety of reasons, there is no question that the telecommunications industry is looking to an era of reduced government intervention and increased reliance on competitive forces. Indeed, the federal government has taken steps to ensure that its efforts at deregulation are not supplanted by state and local reregulation by affirming that the lifting of certain regulatory burdens is an exercise of federal preemption under the provisions of the Commerce Clause of the Constitution, which grants exclusive provenance over interstate commerce to the federal government.

The most striking example of such evolution will be found in federal legislation that sharply restricts the ability of local governments to impose program or channel utilization requirements on cable system operators. Whereas is has been the custom for a city to decree the required composition of a cable system by ordinance, including the number of channels to be devoted to noncommercial services, such as education, the new legislation precludes such action by limiting the ability to extract concessions of this nature to the bargaining process that precedes the granting of a franchise. While an applicant for a cable franchise might use the offer of maximum educational services to obtain the valued approval of the city, the city can no longer require the applicant to offer the specified services as a condition of submitting its application.

In contrast, action by the Federal Communications Commission to eliminate restrictions on the use of broadcast subcarriers (an ordinarily invisible or inaudible portion of the broadcast signal that, through use of a converter attached to the receiving television or radio, can be used to transmit entirely separate programming or data) by noncommercial as well as by commerical stations affords a new opportunity for the development of instructional services that could not justify use of an open-broadcast channel. Thus, the deregulation of telecommunications is already having the effect of increasing the options available for the delivery of educational services. The growing diversity of technologies and the need of operators to develop constituencies for their use have generated considerable potential for use of these vehicles by postsecondary education, especially for services aimed at adult audiences.

The negative potential of deregulation for delivery of educational services lies in the fact that the regulatory framework has afforded protected use of certain parts of the electronic spectrum to educational institutions and other instructional users. A policy of deregulation must therefore be tempered by a strong commitment to the public interest theory if the protection currently afforded to noncommerical educational users is to be preserved. While it is doubtful that the deregulation of telecommunications will eliminate this protection entirely, erosion remains altogether possible.

At the same time that government policies appear to be loosening the regulatory grip on telecommunications, the degree of regulatory oversight over postsecondary education appears to be increasing, although at the state rather than at the federal level. Most states have long exercised some control over the private colleges and universities that operate within their boundaries, as well as over the funding—and through that the programs—of state-supported institutions. In recent years, this regulatory framework has become more sophisticated as states have reacted to a number of influences supportive of a closer supervisory role. These influences include increased demands for public accountability and consumer protection, rationalization of the substantial commitment of increasingly scarce public funds required to deliver postsecondary education, and concern over the need to protect existing institutions from what some view as the depredations of entities that do not have to bear the same facility and resource burdens of domestic schools. As already noted, a "television college" does not need the libraries and other costly facilities required for resident instruction.

With the growth and increased visibility of telecommunications-based delivery systems, the states are showing increased concern not only over outside institutions whose electronic transmissions cross their boundaries but over noninstitutional providers that operate outside traditional frameworks. As some businesses seek to extend their internal educational programs beyond their own employees, and others gear up specifically to provide adult learning services, there is a growing belief that an entirely separate cadre of providers operating within a state but outside its regulatory framework is evolving. The capabilities of telecommunications-based instruction, particularly for large firms that have plants and offices in many states, raise the specter of multistate instructional systems that can escape the oversight of the agencies empowered by law to supervise this function. As the ability to transform all forms of learning into college credit equivalents increases, and the number of institutions designed to do just that increases, the distinction between credit and noncredit programs is fast becoming irrelevant.

Creation of Multistate Delivery Systems and Questions of Control

The critical policy issue arising from the emergence of telecommunications-based instructional delivery systems concerns the question of how to regulate and control such services. Historically, as noted earlier, control of education has been the province of the states, while the Constitution reserves supervision of interstate commerce to the federal government. Telecommunications-based systems, whether based on open-broadcast television, cable, direct broadcast satellites, computer networks, and any of a number of other existing or emerging technologies, inherently ignore political boundaries. Who then has the right to regulate such services, and does the assertion of such a right preclude its exercise by others? The potential for a conflict between federal and state powers is very real, and it is exacerbated by possible conflicts between the states, especially if the delivery system relies on approval in a state with a relatively lenient licensure law.

One possible outcome is federal preemption of the power to regulate and approve interstate delivery of postsecondary education via telecommunications. Alternatively, the accrediting community and state agencies responsible for the licensing of postsecondary education could develop alternative ways of dealing with interstate delivery that would eliminate the necessity of separate approvals in each jurisdiction. While the framework for such a system remains to be defined, one likely approach involves increased reliance on accreditation for distance-learning programs, with the provider's home state having primary responsibility for ensuring the requisite protection and reliability. This would allow a provider of telecommunications-based instruction to seek approval through one state authorizing agency and accreditation through one regional body. So long as that approval was granted through agreed-upon procedures and standards, the service could be delivered in any state where the agreement was in effect, and learners in that state would be afforded the same protection as to quality and rights as students in the state where the approval was issued.

A joint project on Assessing Long-Distance Learning via Telecommunications (Project ALLTELL) by the State Higher Education Executive Officers Association and the Council on Postsecondary Accreditation is seeking to create a framework for such interstate and interregional cooperation. The success of Project ALLTELL and subsequent efforts will in no small measure determine the degree to which postsecondary education will be able to exploit the potential of telecommunications technology.

Conclusion

The public policies that guide and affect telecommunications and postsecondary education are different in both derivation and direction. Telecommunications, which historically have been subject to stringent regulation, are undergoing a transformation that involves an enormous expansion of technology in a policy environment that looks towards deregulation limited only by the technical parameters of physical interference. In contrast, postsecondary education is moving towards increasing regulation as recognition grows of the need to guide the allocation of resources and the availability of services.

The overriding public policy considerations for postsecondary education during the remainder of the twentieth century are likely to revolve around work force development, productivity, and retraining for the information society. Underlying this emphasis, however, a growing thread of interest in ensuring that the American people have the knowledge and information necessary to fulfill their roles as citizens and as participants is the framing of public policy.

The confluence of telecommunications and postsecondary education will result in a new set of policies that increasingly are based on an evolving marketplace approach, which will be punctuated by the evolution of interstate agreements for the approval of delivery systems operating on regional and national (and perhaps international) bases. The outlines of such agreements are already becoming apparent as institutional, state, and accrediting agency leaders seek to develop a framework for these programs while they are still in their infancy.

The absence of coherent government policies on the interface between education and telecommunications may not have been so bad after all. Perhaps we are fortunate in having started with a relatively clean slate, enabling the states, the federal government, the institutions, and the telecommunications entities to work together to design the kinds of systems—and with them the appropriate controls and safeguards—necessary both to protect the interests of the public and to encourage the use of new technologies in meeting the needs of a rapidly changing society.

References

General Education Provisions Act §432, 20 U.S.C. §1232A (1983).

Goldstein, M. B. "Federal Policy Issues Affecting Instructional Television at the Postsecondary Level." In M. Kressel (Ed.), *Adult Learning and Public Broadcasting*. Washington, D.C.: American Association of Community and Junior Colleges, 1980.

Public Law 89–329, as amended, 20 U.S.C. §1001 *et seq.*

Michael B. Goldstein is a partner in the Washington, D.C., law firm of Dow, Lohnes, & Albertson. Former associate vice-chancellor for urban and governmental affairs and associate professor of urban sciences at the University of Illinois–Chicago and former assistant city administrator and director of university relations in the Office of the Mayor, City of New York, he now chairs the Education Law Committee of the Federal Bar Association.

Continuing workplace education in the form of training and
retraining is the key to employment security for American
workers in the information age. Labor unions, like colleges
and universities and other elements of society, must be
prepared to change with the times.

America's Changing Workplace:
The Challenge Ahead

Glenn E. Watts

Recently, U.S. Senator Paul Tsongas (1982, p. 250) offered a bit of rational philosophy for a nation that is now in the midst of what is arguably the greatest economic and societal transition in history, the shift from the industrial age to the information age: "In a time when the shortcut and the short term seem to be the guiding priorities in business and government, we should remember that our task is to mold the future."

America's history shows that past generations have been able to mold the future. Society's shift from the agricultural to the industrial age occasioned a period of unparalleled growth and prosperity for the United States. Machines began to perform tasks that had previously been accomplished by manual labor. America became a nation of factories that achieved the highest productivity standards in the world. In many ways, the industrial revolution coincided with the American revolution and with the transformation of the United States from a colonial infant into an industrial giant.

The current transition in the United States from an industrial-based to an information-based economy represents a crucial challenge to all sectors of society, including higher education and labor. Nowhere is this transition more evident than in the American workplace. Futurists estimate that by 1985 75 percent of all jobs will involve computers in some way. Human resources will replace natural resources as mainstays of the knowledge-intensive society.

P. J. Tate, M. Kressel (Eds.). *The Expanding Role of Telecommunications in Higher Education.*
New Directions for Higher Education, no. 44. San Francisco: Jossey-Bass, December 1983.

Information, which in the words of American futurist Alvin Toffler (Toffler, 1980, p. 351) "can never be exhausted," will become the basic raw material. To a great extent, the future success of unionism in the United States will depend on the ability of unions to adapt to this turbulent and changing work environment.

To grasp the magnitude of the information explosion, consider these statistics: in 1975, there were approximately 500,000 computers in the world. By 1980, there were 3.1 million, and it is estimated that by 1985 there will be more than 10 million (Botkin and others, 1982). In 1977, only some fifty stores nationwide actively catered to the computer buff. Today, more than 10,000 such stores compete for this ever growing market. During this decade, the electronics business will become a $400 billion venture, making it the largest business in the world (Naisbitt, 1982).

No one is more cognizant of the rapid and dramatic changes sweeping the American workplace than the members of the Communications Workers of America (CWA). One of the largest trade unions in the American labor movement, the CWA represents more than 650,000 workers in more than 900 chartered locals across the country. CWA members work in both public and private sectors in more than 10,000 American communities, where they perform a variety of tasks, almost all of which involve information processing in one form or another.

While union membership has become diversified in recent years, the CWA continues to hold the distinction of being the largest telecommunications union in the world. A CWA member can be a telephone operator, a cable splicer, a computer operator, a telephone installer, a service technician, a manufacturing plant technician, or a dispatching clerk. In the Bell System alone, the CWA represents workers with more than 800 different job titles. CWA represents more than 60,000 public sector workers, as well as health care workers, entertainers, journalists, and others who work in communications-related capacities.

Because CWA members are literally on the cutting edge of the technological revolution that is bringing dramatic changes to the American workplace, the union understands the realities of this changing environment. Foremost in its leaders' minds is an awareness that all sectors in society must change. The way in which business, labor, government, and academia anticipate and prepare for the realities of the information society will determine how we mold the future and whether the United States will continue to be the world's technological standard-bearer.

In an effort to anticipate future trends and to prepare members for a rapidly changing workplace, the CWA created a Committee on the Future, the first such union committee of its type, at its 1981 convention. The committee was charged with exploring what living and working in the information age would mean to American workers in particular and to society in general.

Social forecaster John Naisbitt (1982, p. 95) contends that success in the information age requires "nothing less than all of us reconceptualizing our roles." Through its research, the committee sought to begin such a reconceptualization. The fourteen-member committee spent almost two years developing a scenario for the future of the union and its members. During that period, committee members devoted hundreds of hours to research, reading countless articles, books, and papers and receiving comments from a diverse group of experts from business, labor, government, and education. The committee interviewed union leaders and surveyed rank-and-file members to identify possible long-term goals, strategic options, and priorities for the union.

The focus throughout was on anticipating evolving trends and acting accordingly. The CWA wants to be in a position of taking action that will enhance the ability of its members to prosper in the information age, not to be in the position of merely reacting to workplace crises brought on largely by lack of foresight and proper planning for the future. In reporting its findings to the CWA membership at a special union convention, the committee emphasized this need for action and noted that the union's attempt to anticipate and adapt to the future was not being taken a moment too soon: "The information age, which every day becomes more evident to all of us, has been with us for twenty-five years and is acquiring an ever-increasing momentum. Many people and many institutions have become aware of this new era when it was already too late. It is all too evident now to the auto workers and the steel workers, for example, that the industrial age is on the wane. These unions are acting heroically to protect their members, aid their ailing industries, and help their members retool and adjust to change — but they are in the unfortunate position of reacting. CWA's commitment must be to act and plan now to control our destiny" (Communications Workers of America, 1983, p. 9).

As the committee's scenario developed, it became clear that the evolving information age holds the potential for new and interesting careers for millions of Americans. That promise is tempered by the potential of the new society to create new and serious workplace problems, including problems of stress and work-related health hazards. An example from the telecommunications industry offers a glimpse of the special brand of tension and job stress associated with the new wave of technology: In the past, the main source of job stress for telephone operators was pressure from numerous switchboard supervisors, who measured an operator's performance by the number of calls that he or she handled during a given period of time. The resulting tension was often overpowering for the employee. Today, the human badgering has been replaced by buzzing computers. As a result of new technology, computerized measuring sticks for job performance are rapidly being introduced into the workplace. The performance of telephone operators is still measured; the difference is that their performance is now being measured by computers. The end result is that stress remains a part of the job.

Studies are beginning to reveal that office work, which most people categorize as safe, clean, and generally free of stress, can involve health hazards and alarming levels of job-related stress. For example, the Framingham Heart Study found that female clerical and secretarial workers developed coronary disease at nearly twice the rate of other female workers (Haynes and Feinbleib, 1980). Less than ideal lighting arrangements, poorly designed chairs used for long periods of time, and pollution of office air by irritating fumes from office machines are now recognized as potential health hazards to office workers.

One of the most serious problems of the information age office involves the potential health hazards associated with video display terminals (VDTs). The complaints of VDT operators most frequently consist of visual and postural problems—irritation and soreness of the eyes and discomforts related to the neck and back. After spending several hours in front of a VDT, many workers are prone to experience dull and lingering headaches. In many ways, video display terminals represent the clearest example of how modern technology brings its own type of stress and strain to the workplace. Health problems associated with VDTs and other modern office equipment are of particular concern to the CWA, since hundreds of thousands of its members work in environments that require continual use of these instruments.

In the committee's search for future trends, it became increasingly evident that work patterns in the year 2000 will be very different from work patterns today. The next two to three decades have the potential to produce serious disruptions and dislocations in the American work force. Such basic industries as steel, auto, and rubber manufacturing will continue to decline, just as the American textile and shoe industries have already done. For American workers, this steady decline translates into lost jobs—lost to foreign manufacturers in many instances. This decline in traditional industries is accompanied by the likelihood that an increasing amount of industrial work will be performed by robots. The robot factory is already a reality today.

As the information age becomes more firmly entrenched, new technology will permit many tasks to be done both at home and at widely dispersed work locations. Jobs created by new technology will require increased knowledge and decision-making capabilities on the part of workers. Thus, workers will require increased amounts of training and retraining in order to satisfy the demands of ever changing technology.

It has become clear that the normal life cycle of many existing jobs is getting shorter. In the past, it was possible to train for a job and expect the job requirement to remain relatively stable for at least five to ten years. Today, jobs and the skills and knowledge required to perform them are evolving much more rapidly. Hence, a much broader range of abilities is needed to keep pace with these changes. It is clear, therefore, that the key to a CWA member's long-term employment security and career development is the member's acquired work skills and knowledge.

These realities are reflected in the emphasis placed on the committee's final report on worker training. The report makes the need for continuing workplace education its highest priority: "The key to employment security is through training and retraining" (Communications Workers of America, 1983, p. 7). To underline the importance that it placed on continuing workplace education, the Committee on the Future recommended and gained overwhelming approval for the establishment of employee career development and training programs. These training efforts are to be established through negotiations with the major employers with whom the union holds collective bargaining agreements, and they will be jointly administered by the union and the employer. As new collective bargaining negotiations are held with each major employer, the CWA intends to make the establishment of career and development training programs one of its top bargaining priorities.

The intent of these employee retraining programs is to maximize existing company, union, educational, and public sector resources. Each training program is intended to build on the employer's existing efforts and to improve their effectiveness by introducing new and better approaches and techniques. In this way, the union will be in a better position to anticipate changes in the workplace and work force requirements and to initiate early corrective action on behalf of its members.

This training and retraining initiative is designed to assist workers who find themselves in a situation where they need help in order to keep their job or find a new one. A key ingredient of this program will be the CWA's support of community colleges and vocational and technical schools in their development of courses, some of which are directly related to the development of information industry skills. Examples of courses where areas of need are probable include marketing, programming, word processing, basic mathematics, computer literacy, typing, design, computer installation and maintenance, and problem analysis and problem solving.

In recent years, several innovative training and retraining programs have been initiated to assist workers displaced as a result of technological change or plant closings. The largest such program was established in July 1982 as part of an agreement between the Ford Motor Company and the United Auto Workers (UAW). The jointly administered company-funded employee development and training program provides workers with what one UAW official termed a "vehicle for survival." Since the program was implemented, some 4,000 displaced workers have enrolled in training and retraining projects at twelve of Ford's sixty major auto plants. Another 4,000 have applied for tuition aid assistance. Program administrators hope to have projects implemented at all sixty Ford plants eventually (CWA News, 1983, p. 13).

Another massive training and retraining effort has taken place in Wayne County, Michigan following the layoff in 1980 of some 7,000 workers from manufacturing plants of Ford, BASF, Dana, and Firestone. In all, sixteen communities banded together to create one of the nation's most successful training and retraining programs. To date, 2,700 workers have graduated from the program, and an astounding 66 percent have been placed in jobs (Communications Workers of America, 1983, p. 13).

The CWA initiated its first retraining and counseling program in spring 1983 in response to the layoff of some 1,500 union members from a Western Electric manufacturing plant near Kansas City. Developed in cooperation with the Compact for Lifelong Educational Opportunities, a consortium of colleges and universities in the Delaware Valley, Pennsylvania, this program was designed to help workers to cope with the stress and trauma of layoffs, offer guidance about retraining opportunies based on assessment of each worker's skills and interests, and assist unemployed CWA members in their search for new jobs. The CWA intends both to expand this program to unemployed members in other locals and to use it as the basis for more extensive programs for employed members.

For the most part, CWA members and other workers in the information industries have emerged from the depressed economic climate of recent years in somewhat better shape than workers in most other segments of the economy. But, while the future of the information and high technology industries appears to be bright and filled with the promise of growth for many decades to come, the Western Electric layoff, the first large-scale layoff that the CWA has encountered, serves as a warning that, without proper long-term vision and planning, these industries and their workers could fall victim to the same maladies that plague the American auto and steel industries today.

To respond to the challenge of increasing pressure from foreign competitors, unions will need to become more innovative and flexible in their approaches. In the telecommunications age, successful unions will have to present a fresh image, offer new kinds of educational services to members, and exemplify a readiness to enter into new alliances for the collective benefit of union members. It is our view that collaborative efforts between management and labor, such as the retraining programs mentioned earlier and the worker participation projects commonly referred to as quality of work life programs are necessary if the United States is to maintain its position as a world leader in the field of advanced technology. If management and labor are locked in a rigid, adversarial relationship, the creative and imaginative atmosphere necessary for problem solving is not likely.

Such innovations as worker participation and retraining programs underscore the importance of long-term planning, which has been a repeated theme throughout this chapter. If American business is to become more competitive in the international market, it must develop more effective long-term strategies and turn away from the preoccupation with the short term, particularly from its preoccupation with short-term profits. Long-term strategies have been a centerpiece of Japanese enterprise since that nation lay in ruins in the aftermath of World War II. Japan's focus on the long term — which often sacrificed the short term — has paid rich dividends as Japanese interests have garnered steadily increasing shares of the world market in automobiles, electronics, and high technology.

Bendix Corporation chairman William Agee reflected this awareness when he noted that "one of the problems in the United States with government and business is the very short-term, expedient approach to problems — this quarter's earnings, this year's budget: 'Get me through the next election or the next board meeting'" (Naisbitt, 1982, p. 81). Economist Lester Thurow (1980, p. 40) offers a blunt warning about the consequences for the United States of a failure on the part of business and government to shift to long-term thinking: "Americans simply will not be able to compete in the modern world of international trade without changes in the way they [have] traditionally operated."

The burgeoning information industry offers a case in point. In the short term, there appears little cause to expect anything other than continued American dominance in this market. In 1980, U.S. companies maintained more than 80 percent of the world computer market (Botkin and others, 1982). But, warning signals on the horizon indicate that the long-term strategies of the Japanese and, surprisingly, the French are taking direct aim at American dominance.

When engineers developed a single computer chip that concentrated 16,000 memory cells, it was considered an engineering feat. In just a few short years, Japanese manufacturers have captured 40 percent of the world market for these devices. Now, a chip has been developed that will hold 64,000 bits of information. Of the initial market for this chip, the Japanese have captured an astounding 70 percent share. A chip that will hold an astonishing 256,000 bits of information is currently under development, and it is the Japanese who are pioneering the research (Botkin and others, 1982).

If the example of the Japanese is not a strong enough argument for the advantages of national strategies and long-term planning, consider French prime Minister Francois Mitterrand's challenge in 1981 to that nation's business leaders: "I want to set before you a challenge: to establish France by 1988 as the world leader in as many sectors of the communications industry as possible" (Botkin and others, 1982, p. 11).

Economist Alan Greenspan contends that national economic policy in the United States is determined not so much by the political party that is in power as by the consensus coming out of the nation's colleges and universities (AFL–CIO, Department of Education, 1980). This notion holds that the general direction of higher education today will significantly influence government and business policies and directions in the coming decade. If this notion is at all accurate, it spells problems for this country's high technology industries in the years ahead vis-à-vis foreign competition.

Japan is producing three times as many engineers as American universities are, despite a population that is only half the size. The demand for computer scientists and electrical engineers in the United States tremendously exceeds the supply coming out of the nation's academic institutions (Botkin and others, 1982). These statistics seem to point to an erosion of American dominance in the high technology industries. Do they mean that American students, workers, business executives, government leaders, and academic institutions are inferior to their foreign counterparts? No. Americans, in the collective sense, remain as capable as the citizens of any other nation. What these statistics reveal is that all elements of American society have suffered from the absence of national strategies for transition to the information age. Other nations have captured increasing shares of world markets at the expense of the United States's preoccupation with the short term. Just as the CWA has attempted to anticipate and prepare for the realities of the information age through its Committee on the Future, business, government, and higher education must also pursue long-range solutions.

In 1862, Congress passed the Morrill Act, which established the land-grant college system and sparked a technological revolution that made the United States the world leader in agriculture. The Morrill Act and the land-grant college system represented a national strategy and a long-term approach to a potential national problem. In early 1983, legislation entitled the High Technology Morrill Act was introduced in Congress. Modeled after the original Morrill Act, this legislation proposed to establish a national grants program to foster technological education. The proposal would provide assistance from the federal government for joint initiatives among private industry, educational institutions, and state governments to strengthen scientific, engineering, and technical education. To qualify for a grant under this measure, an applicant would have to propose a program involving three participants — an educational institution; industry, which would contribute 20 percent of the total cost; and a state government, which would pay another 30 percent. The federal grant would cover the remaining 50 percent.

The High Technology Morrill Act or similarly directed legislation would bolster technological education at all levels. For example, a national commitment of this type could create programs to modernize university laboratory equipment, improve mathematics and science instruction in elementary and secondary schools, provide lifelong education to maintain the technical skills of the present work force, expand technician training at community colleges, establish computer courses in elementary and secondary schools, retrain workers for jobs that require more technical skills, and aid in the establishment of university research and training centers. Programs such as the High Technology Morrill Act should not be viewed as quick solutions. Rather, they must be seen as long-term investments.

Naisbitt (1982, p. 252) offers this interesting perspective on the future: "Those who anticipate the new era will be a quantum leap ahead of those who hold on to the past. If we can learn to make uncertainty our friend, we can achieve much more." The members of the CWA think that long-term strategy represents our nation's best chance for prosperity and security during a period of dramatic technological, economic, and social change. The union has gone to great length and expense to position itself well for the future. Its members have also attempted to share their findings about societal trends with others. We firmly believe that there is a message in this project for all segments of society. The union has produced a public affairs television and radio series entitled

"Rewiring Your World" that brings knowledgeable panelists together for discussions about the potential benefits, costs, and implications of the information age. The series has been viewed by millions of Americans, and it has been critically acclaimed by educators, business leaders, and government officials across the country.

We are serious in our contention that, if we are not prepared to change with the times, we can be overrun by change. We do not wish to imply that our efforts provide all the answers and solutions to the complex workplace of the future or to the problems that such an environment could create. We do insist, however, that exercises of similar scope are essential to the success of businesses, labor unions, governments, and academic institutions in the years ahead.

References

AFL–CIO Department of Education. *Corporate Influence in Economic Education.* Washington, D.C.: AFL–CIO, 1980.

Botkin, J., Dimancescu, D., and Stata, R. *Global Stakes.* New York: Harper & Row, 1982.

Communications Workers of America. *Committee on the Future Report.* Washington, D.C.: Communications Workers of America, 1983.

Communications Workers of America. *CWA News.* February/March 1983, *42* (2), 9–16.

Haynes, S., and Feinbleib, M. "Women, Work, and Coronary Heart Disease: Prospective Findings from the Framingham Heart Study." *American Journal of Public Health,* 1980, *70* (2), 133–141.

Naisbitt, J. *Megatrends.* New York: Warner Books, 1982.

Thurow, L. "The Productivity Problem." *Technology Review,* 1980, *83* (2), 40–51.

Toffler, A. *The Third Wave.* New York: Bantam Books, 1980.

Tsongas, P. *The Road From Here.* New York: Random House, 1982.

Glenn E. Watts is president of the 650,000-member Communications Workers of America, the largest telecommunications union in the world. One of thirty-five union leaders on the AFL–CIO executive council, he also chairs the AFL–CIO's public relations committee, and he was instrumental in the creation of the Labor Institute for Public Affairs.

The editors offer concluding thoughts on the topics treated
in the volume as well as a list of further resources.

Concluding Comments
and Further Resources

Pamela J. Tate
Marilyn Kressel

The chapters in this sourcebook presume that information technologies are here to stay and that colleges and universities can harness them for effective use. As the authors have discussed the variety of issues that university leaders confront, they have briefly mentioned an impressive array of technology-based programs and services developed for diverse groups of learners. Unfortunately, space in which to describe these programs in detail, to report on research in the field of mediated instruction, and to analyze all the issues presented is lacking. Thus, in these concluding comments we will highlight some themes that emerge from the preceding chapters, add others, suggest next steps for colleges and universities in the telecommunications arena, and refer readers to resources that deal more fully with such areas as research, program development, and innovative uses of specific technologies.

It is clear that, while the newer information technologies have not replaced broadcasting, they have captured the public's imagination. Awareness of the flexibility, cost-effectiveness, interactive capability, and portability of the new technologies has increased, and their applications are being explored in institutions of all kinds. Exciting experiments using interactive cable, video-disks, satellites for audio and video teleconferencing, and combinations of several information technologies are now under way. Even with technologies as

P. J. Tate, M. Kressel (Eds.). *The Expanding Role of Telecommunications in Higher Education.*
New Directions for Higher Education, no. 44. San Francisco: Jossey-Bass, December 1983.

new as videotext and teletext (described briefly by Welling in Chapter Three), there are already pilot projects and studies in progress to examine their instructional potential; for example, both San Diego State University and the University of Nebraska, Lincoln, have developed pilot courses to be delivered via videotext and teletext.

However, as we indicated in the Editors' Notes, it is not the novelty of the technologies that should prompt educational institutions to use them. Instead, institutions should consider organizational and academic concerns, such as the learner groups that they are trying to reach or the new administrative systems that they need, and then determine whether technology can help to solve the problem.

Several examples in the instructional area will illustrate this approach. Kirkwood Community College in Cedar Rapids, Iowa, has decided to reach incarcerated adults at the Iowa State Men's Reformatory by offering credit courses and vocational programming through an instructional television fixed service (ITFS) channel. Kirkwood also coordinates programming for one of its cable channels for a consortium of community agencies in Cedar Rapids. Technology is the key to delivering both services.

The To Education the People Consortium model created by Wayne State University in Detroit, which has been adopted by colleges in fifteen other cities, is another example of a program delivered with the aid of technology to a population that is rarely reached by higher education—blue-collar working adults. This program, which allows a working adult to earn a baccalaureate degree in five years, has three thematically integrated components: a weekly class conducted by faculty at the work site, several weekend seminars each semester, and televised course material that can be viewed at home or in libraries and community sites. In this model, the televised courses make it possible for students to take a full-time course load without having to attend classes at a college during their work week.

Handicapped populations have also been well served by programs using technology. For example, closed captioning for the deaf, a form of teletext technology requiring a special decoder on the television receiver, has been effective in serving the needs of the hearing-impaired. Similarly, the use of subcarrier radio—FM frequencies set aside by the Federal Communications Commission—allows visually impaired learners to receive special programming through a decoder on their radio receiver. Central Piedmont Community College in North Carolina provides a reading service as well as GED preparation for the visually impaired over such channels. The Homebound Program at Queensborough Community College in New York is another exemplary model that uses telephone technology to serve handicapped students who cannot attend classes on campus. Fifty classrooms at the college are equipped with telephone conference units, and a two-way hookup between these units and telephone receivers or purchased speaker phones in the homes of the handicapped allows students to participate in on-campus classes.

These illustrations of how technology can help an institution to reach underserved and handicapped populations should not obscure the important point that Dirr makes in Chapter Two—colleges and universities have become heavy users of television for regular on-campus students. In Chapters One and Four, Tucker and Gillespie make a related point about microcomputers— institutions of higher education are discovering that they can be useful in all areas of campus life, especially when they can be linked with other technologies. Clearly, the array of options available to colleges and universities as they consider using communications technologies is expanding, as well as the problems that technology can help to solve.

Critical Issues

But administrators and faculty need to confront several critical issues before deciding in which directions their institutions should be heading in relation to telecommunications. First, while suppliers of communications technologies emphasize the increased access to postsecondary education that their technologies make possible, their assumption stands in need of careful examination. Do telecommunications technologies necessarily make postsecondary education programs more available to previously unserved people? Some disturbing facts tend to indicate that they do not, except in special programs like those just described. Like most continuing education programs, telecourses and other forms of technology-based instruction tend to attract those who are already inclined to pursue additional education—those with previous educational experience who can afford to pay. As Lewis (1982, p. 62) points out in his analysis of seventy telecommunications-based model programs, most of the learners served by the programs that he examined were "white high school graduates between twenty-five and thirty-four years of age, employed more than thirty-five hours per week with annual family incomes of $15,000 to $25,000." The ability of technology-based instruction to reach disadvantaged adults appears to be more a function of the outreach efforts that institutions conduct and of the cost of the programs for learners than of the accessibility that technology makes possible.

Cost of instruction clearly relates to issues of equity and access. A student enrolled in a telecourse does not benefit from a reduction in the institution's tuition fee, although the telecourse may cost the institution less than a classroom-based course would. If the student takes the telecourse via cable rather than via open-broadcast television, the student bears the additional cost of the cable hookup. Indeed, the costs of all hardware necessary to participate in learning via technology—cable hookup, teletext or videotext decoder, videocassette recorder, speaker telephone, videodisk playback machine, or personal computer—are usually borne by the student. If telecommunications are truly to increase access to education for disadvantaged learners, these financial obstacles must be overcome. If solutions are not found, telecommunications delivery systems will continue to offer primarily middle-class learners a much wider variety of educational options and thereby widen the gap between what many have called the information-rich and the information-poor.

No discussion of the implications of technology-based delivery systems would be complete without mention of the complex legal maze surrounding the field. As institutions develop the capacity both to disseminate course materials via satellite, computer, and cable and to bring in a vast range of course materials generated elsewhere, the issues of state licensure and accreditation of institutional programs discussed by Goldstein in Chapter Five become increasingly complicated. As course material is transmitted from one institution to students and institutions across state borders, where does the degree-granting authority lie? Who signs off on the academic caliber of the programs? How is eligibility for federal funds determined for students enrolled in these programs?

In recognition of these issues, the Fund for the Improvement of Postsecondary Education awarded a grant to the State Higher Education Executive Officers and the Council on Postsecondary Accreditation to develop a national framework for assessing educational programs delivered through electronic media. The emphasis was placed on eliminating interstate barriers while preserving the critical elements of consumer protection and quality assurance. This project is also examining the complex issues that arise from federal preemption of broadcasting and from the deregulation of alternative electronic media, such as cable, satellites, and other technologies that inherently ignore jurisdictional lines.

Another important issue in the instructional area is the need to maintain quality in technology-based programs and the role of faculty in such maintenance. As long as courses were developed by local faculty for use on campus closed-circuit television systems, control over course content remained in faculty hands. However, with the proliferation of nationally distributed telecourses (one recent inventory identified more than 200 telecourses in national circulation) and audio courses, faculty often find themselves in the role of reviewer or refiner rather than creator of course materials. They are, therefore, understandably concerned not only about the quality of the courses and their relevance to the particular college curriculum but also about the standardization of content that these courses portend. Rather than dismissing these concerns as simple faculty resistance to technology in particular or to innovation in general, it is critical to recognize that legitimate questions have been raised by the rapid growth of the telecourse business—such as the trend toward standardized courses and centralization of course production. Many institutions have found successful ways of addressing these concerns by demonstrating to faculty that they can continue to play a key role in the instructional process although a telecourse is being used. In fact, several studies have found that, when faculty have had experience teaching a telecourse, their concerns about quality and control tend to diminish. It becomes clear to them that they are not being replaced by technology and that they are free to supplement the prepackaged readings and exercises or to substitute their own print materials, much as they already do with study guides and examination questions supplied by textbook publishers.

But in the computer courseware business, prospects for faculty involvement may not be so promising. According to participants at a meeting jointly sponsored by the Modern Language Association and the National Endowment for the Humanities on the potential instructional uses of computers in high school and undergraduate curricula (Desruisseaux, 1983, p. 10), "many institutions do not have the resources to develop their own programs, and faculty members who might be interested in working on such projects are often discouraged from doing so because the work is not recognized as scholarship."

Theodore Ricks, director of electronic publishing at Harper & Row, (Magarrell, 1983, p. 9), estimates that "about 300 hours of programming are needed to create one hour of computerized instruction, and the development of a course for use on computers costs $50,000 to $100,000 and takes three to five years. Current prices for a single copy of a computerized course range from $50 to $500, . . . but in the next three years, increased volume should bring the price range down to $30 to $50." These production costs, like the production costs for nationally distributed telecourses, are frequently prohibitive for an institution unless it collaborates with industry or other colleges, receives foundation support, or uses development capital that it hopes to replace later.

In the meantime, 620 commercial manufacturers of computer courseware in this country have already produced nearly 2,500 educational software products geared primarily to the elementary and secondary education markets. They have not yet moved aggressively into the postsecondary market, where demand for courseware is outstripping supply, especially as the number of personal computers grows. A survey by one marketing research company estimated that the average number of microcomputers per college has increased from six in 1980 to forty-five in 1983; this figure is expected to grow to 141 in 1985. Faculty who attempt to use computer courseware either cannot find appropriate or compatible software, or they complain that much of the courseware is simply not high-quality. Further, there are no guidelines to help educators assess the effectiveness of courseware with students. The absence of quality control makes it virtually impossible to discern the relative strengths and weaknesses of computer software programs without extensive investigation by each faculty member who is considering their use. Fortunately, such organizations as EDUCOM, a consortium of colleges and universities dedicated to the effective application of computer technologies, and the CONDUIT project at the University of Iowa are seeking to remedy this situation. These organizations select, evaluate, and distribute course materials that meet certain pedagogical and technical standards.

Most discussions of the issues surrounding the introduction of communications technologies in higher education focus on the applications or on the need to train students to work in information industries. Less attention is paid to the role of higher education as (Schiller, 1982, p. 1) "a significant supplier of education in a telecommunications environment." Schiller's point is an important one for institutional leaders to consider. If higher education is to remain a central institution in society's system of educational providers, he argues (p. 2) it must have access to or control over the "educational distribution/transmission and delivery system — the conduit in a telecommunications environment. Second, it must be able to shape or control educational materials or courseware — the content — in a telecommunications environment."

As several of our authors indicate, the private sector has always controlled access to the conduit. For example, except for the twenty-eight channels reserved for instructional television and the channels recently reserved on local cable systems for educational access, educational institutions have had to depend on the goodwill of commercial broadcasters for free air time. Although many stations and cable companies committed to public service have established nonprofit rates, the basic premise is that educational institutions are one of many paying customers. With the recent cutbacks in federal funding for the public broadcasting system, educational institutions and other nonprofit groups find that free access to broadcast time has become even more limited. This underscores that higher education institutions need to become involved in the formulation of telecommunications policy.

The degree to which colleges and universities can play a central role in shaping the content of education in a telecommunications environment should be a matter of vital concern to institutional leaders. It is crucial for institutions to provide opportunities for training, release time, and other incentives that will encourage faculty to produce technology-based learning materials, to become experienced in using and evaluating software, and to work collaboratively with other suppliers of courseware, such as the publishing industry. In fact, publishers, such as Theodore Ricks of Harper & Row, are calling on universities for assistance in developing courses for computer-aided instruction — and are asking universities to offer faculty time, recognition, and a share of royalties in exchange for their contribution.

But, as higher education enters into such partnerships, a number of important issues must be confronted. As Gillespie emphasizes in Chapter Four, institutions need to develop policies on copyright and royalties on educational materials developed by faculty. For example, when a commercial manufacturer of courseware assesses the market potential of certain subject areas, then hires faculty as private consultants to assist in the development of course content and design, who owns the copyright, and who gets the royalties? Who decides which courses and curricula will be developed and which will be neglected? How can colleges and universities become more involved in the decision making about such matters? How can they do more than simply react after the fact to the menu of software programs and hardware produced? Can effective partnerships be established with commercial producers in ways that maintain the autonomy and integrity of higher education? As Knapper (1982, p. 88) cautions, "it is likely that if educators fail to come to grips with technological advances, instructional technology will be left to those outside the academic world, including those who may well attempt to develop instructional systems according to criteria that are more commercial than educational."

Next Steps

Our authors have demonstrated that colleges and universities have already become heavily involved in the use of a variety of communications technologies for the delivery of instruction to on-campus and off-campus learners, for administrative and scholarly purposes, and for the provision of services to industry and the general public. But, it appears that few educators have taken an active role at the local, state, and national levels in shaping the policies that will create the telecommunications environment of the future.

In late May 1983, the Federal Communications Commission (FCC) decided that eight of the twenty-eight channels reserved exclusively for educational purposes since 1963 would be reallocated to pay-television broadcasters. This ruling represented a compromise between commercial operators, who had asked the FCC to reallocate more than half of the channels because they claimed that nonprofit groups had underutilized them, and nonprofit organizations, such as universities and hospitals, which opposed any reallocation. The seven education associations that make up the Joint Committee on Telecommunications organized a strong campaign to prevent the reallocation, and according to Scully (1983, p. 7) more than twenty university leaders wrote to the chairman of the FCC to oppose the change. But, even though educators could demonstrate that there had been a substantial increase in instructional and cultural programming on the designated channels by colleges and universities in recent years, higher education's case was only strong enough to reduce the number of channels to be reallocated. As a result, almost one third of the channels that had been reserved for educational use since 1963 were reassigned to commercial operators. Although the FCC made provisions to assure licenses to universities that already held instructional television fixed service (ITFS) licenses and to universities that applied for licenses before May 26, 1983, the reallocation decision clearly represents an erosion of the principle of reserving public service frequencies.

A historical comparison is important here. Twenty years ago, higher education was in an offensive and creative position. It argued that educational access needed to be expanded through the vehicle of ITFS channels. Today, higher education is in a defensive position. Now, it can only argue that some channels should still be reserved for education use. Higher education must take an offensive position with regard to new technologies. For example, higher education has opportunities to play a role in shaping the ways in which direct broadcast satellite (DBS) technology is applied. Technical improvements have placed ownership of a satellite receiving dish within the reach of the individual consumer, and DBS will soon be able to provide radio, television, and data-transmission services directly to private homes, businesses, and other institutions. But, unless higher education joins with other nonprofit groups to advocate the reserved frequency principle for satellite transponder space, it is unlikely that a portion of the DBS service will be made available for nonprofit and educational uses. Instead, commercial operators will control DBS, and higher education will be forced to pay handsomely for satellite time.

An equally significant area of policy development has emerged with the divestiture of AT&T. Since it is expected that the divestiture will result in sharp rate increases, all organizations that depend on telephone lines for their transmission of data, voice, or video will be dramatically affected. As Lewis (1982, p. 66) points out, "audio teleconferencing, which has been one of the most cost-efficient technologies for serving groups of learners dispersed over large geographical areas, could conceivably become much less affordable for many postsecondary organizations." Yet, Susan Fratkin, Director of Special Programs for the National Associations of State Universities and Land-Grant Colleges (1982, p. 3) has noted that, when a number of legislative proposals were introduced in the House and the Senate to alter the settlement, colleges and universities,which Fratkin describes as "big users of the telephone" were notably absent: "Regulators, competitors, communications workers, consumer groups, and Congress are the ones raising the serious questions about the AT&T settlement." Fratkin argues that it is essential for institutions of higher education to make themselves heard.

Cable television franchising provides another illustration of the low level of educator involvement in the shaping of policy — this time at the local level. Although a number of institutions in recent years have acted either through consortia or individually to secure educational access channels on new cable systems in their community, many others, especially where cable systems were created in the early 1970s, failed to see the potential of cable and did not influence the politics of local franchise awards. As a result, for the period of the franchise — often fifteen years — they lost the opportunity for free educational access channels, access to equipment and production facilities, and other free services that newer cable systems have the technical capacity to provide, such as institutional loops that allow several branch campuses of a university to interact.

Institutions must also pay more attention to cable legislation at the national level. During spring and fall, 1983, bills relating to cable were introduced both in the Senate and in the House. The National Federation of Local Cable Programmers (NFLCP) spearheaded a campaign against the Senate bill, because it contained provisions that they believe will weaken the position of nonprofit and community groups in relation to the cable companies. Higher Education should be aware of the NFLCP campaign to change this bill, and it should follow legislative deliberations on other bills to determine whether community and educational interests are being served or sacrificed.

Welling (1983, p. 56) clearly articulates the need for a strategic, coordinated response to telecommunications policy on the part of higher education: "Missing today in policy making for new technologies is the concept that a certain level of capacity should be reserved in each service for the development of those activities that support public, as distinct from private, interests . . . With rare exceptions and in stark contrast to the political energy focused on the FCC in the early days of radio and television, little is being done by colleges and universities to excite the imaginations of legislators, regulators, or government administrators about the potential of new technologies to support the goals of public education. There is in fact little organized support from the higher education community for even the established public telecommunications services. Very few educators took the trouble to testify on behalf of federal financing for public broadcasting in 1975 and 1981 . . . What is needed is a new initiative on the part of university people both locally and nationally to insist upon educational applications of the new technologies, so that education won't end up as simply one of the paying customers of a nationwide electronic communications system. Educators must find their vision and their voices to speak again with the kind of force that led forty years ago to a public policy that recognized the promise of their role in broadcasting."

One way in which colleges and universities can work to influence policy is through their national professional organizations. The Joint Committee on Telecommunications mentioned earlier was formed by the American Association of Community and Junior Colleges, the American Association for Higher Education, the American Association of State Colleges and Universities, the American Council on Education, the Council of Independent Colleges, the National University Continuing Education Association, and the National Association of State Universities and Land Grant Colleges. Each of these associations has a committee or task force related to education and telecommunications that provides information on important policy developments and practices in this field. (See the Further Resources in this sourcebook for the addresses and telephone numbers of these organizations.) Institutional leaders must become part of this network of information and action.

Colleges and universities must also become involved at the state level. Forming a statewide task force on telecommunications and higher education, like the Ohio committee that Welling mentions in Chapter Three, could be the first step in this direction. Other institutions are taking such steps. For example, in fall 1982, the dean of continuing education at the University of Missouri was assessing a number of statewide plans for education and communications technologies in order to submit a proposal to the Missouri state legislature for funding a statewide effort. Participants in Alaska, Colorado, Georgia, Indiana, Kentucky, Minnesota, Nebraska, Ohio, Pennsylvania, South Carolina, and Virginia have already been in contact with the University of Missouri, and a list of individuals directing such statewide projects will be developed after the Missouri study is complete ("Study of Statewide Plans," 1982, p. 12). We are also aware of statewide plans for cable in Kansas and Massachusetts. These initiatives are promising, and they should be investigated by colleges and universities.

Keeping abreast of the policy, financial, and service implications of the evolving new technologies is a problem for educational institutions. In the 1950s and 1960s, attention was focused primarily on television, radio, and the telephone. Today, a much wider range of information technologies and providers has to be tracked. Ironically, as the technologies themselves become more portable, interactive, and user-friendly, the confusion about them increases. For this reason, colleges and universities must take part in the networks that provide information and technical assistance.

Research

Higher education also needs to develop the research on learning through new technologies. Although a great deal of research on learning styles, barriers to adult learning, and the effectiveness of instructional television and radio has already been done, little is known about the effectiveness of various computer courseware packages. And, as combinations of technologies become more common, we will need more information about which combinations enhance learning. For example, audio teleconferencing has been used to deliver instruction at several institutions, such as Rio Salado Community College in Phoenix. Now, slow-scan freeze-frame television is being used to expand some of these programs. Does the introduction of a video component, which substantially adds to the cost, increase the learning outcomes for students? Is there a correlation between the production quality of video-based course material and the retention of course content by learners? Some literature suggests that as the production itself becomes more professional, the student becomes less likely to focus on the course content.

In evaluating the effectiveness of instructional technology, Knapper (1982, p. 84) stresses that questions need to be raised "about the instructional goals, the types of learning it is intended to foster, the sorts of students involved, and the environmental constraints imposed by time, distance, money, availability of teaching staff." In other words, instructional effectiveness is a complex concept, and it can encompass a host of variables, including "learning speed and time, costs, students' attitudes, ability to respond to individual differences between students, and quality of the learning experience in addition to the amount of learning that takes place.

Knapper (1982) makes it clear that a number of problems will have to be overcome before communications technologies can live up to their promise for enhancing learning. For example, Knapper notes that, while technology advocates claimed that programmed instruction and computer-assisted instruction would enable faculty to keep detailed records of student feedback that could be used to improve the quality of the materials, this has rarely happened in practice. "Furthermore," he adds, "in the case of some technology-based systems, such as videodisk, technical constraints make it very difficult to change the basic teaching material once it has been recorded (Knapper, 1982, p. 86). Both Knapper and other authors raise fundamental questions about the gap between the claims for the ability of technology to enrich and individualize learning and the actual results achieved. Further research in these areas should be encouraged and supported by higher education, government, and the private sector.

Conclusion

These are just a few of the many complex issues related to telecommunications and postsecondary education that our authors have raised. The pace of technological innovation, the high stakes for colleges and universities, students' increasing familiarity with technology, and the rapid transition to an information society described by Watts in Chapter Six—all these forces press for the development of comprehensive approaches to telecommunications by higher education. Orientation and training programs for faculty and administrators need to be established, organizational structures need to be reexamined in light of the introduction of communications technologies on campus, and networks of information and technical assistance need to be fostered. Ways of integrating voice, video, and data communications into a single system that includes research, administrative, and instructional functions need to be devised so that institutions can operate more cost-effectively. And, strategies must be developed for influencing policy and increasing financing of telecommunications delivery systems so that learners in all socioeconomic groups can participate in higher education.

Communications technologies hold great promise for many areas of university life, and they are an important part of the preparation of students for leadership roles in the information society. But, without careful planning by universities, caution about the temptation to make technology an end, not a means, and more active participation in the development of policy and courseware, colleges and universities will increasingly find themselves on the periphery of society's system of educational providers.

References

Desruisseaux, P. "Lack of Computer Programs Slows Use, Humanists Say." *Chronicle of Higher Education,* February 23, 1983, p. 10.
Fratkin, S. "The Breakup of AT&T: Implications for Colleges and Universities." *Telescan,* 1982, *1* (6), 3.
Knapper, C. K. (Ed.). *Expanding Learning Through New Communications Technologies.* New Directions for Teaching and Learning, no. 9. San Francisco: Jossey-Bass, 1982.
Lewis, R. J. *Meeting Learners' Needs Through Telecommunications: A Directory and Guide to Programs.* Washington, D.C.: Center for Learning and Telecommunications, American Association for Higher Education, 1982.

104

Magarrell, J. "Microcomputers Proliferate on College Campuses." *Chronicle of Higher Education,* April 6, 1983, p. 9.

Schiller, D. "Higher Education in the Information Society." Address to CAEL-Ohio University New Connections for Learning conference, May 1982.

Scully, M. G. "FCC May Turn Over Instructional Channels to Pay TV Operators." *Chronicle of Higher Education,* March 23, 1983, p. 7.

"Study of Statewide Plans for Technology Underway." *Telescan,* 1982, *2* (7), 12.

Welling, J. "Setting Communications Policy: Where Are the Colleges?" *Chronicle of Higher Education,* April 27, 1983, p. 56.

Further Resources

The lists of organizations and printed sources in this chapter are intended not to exhaust the possibilities but to serve as a guide to some of those sources and to open the door to additional resource material.

General Organizations

Marilyn Kressel, Director
Center for Learning and Telecommunications
American Association for Higher Education
One Dupont Circle, Suite 600
Washington, D. C. 20036
(202) 293-6440

American Council on Education
One Dupont Circle
Washington, D.C. 20036
(202) 833-4700

Council of Independent Colleges and Universities
One Dupont Circle
Washington, D.C. 20036
(202) 466-7320

James Zigerell, Staff Director
Instructional Telecommunications Consortium
American Association of Community and Junior Colleges
One Dupont Circle, Suite 410
Washington, D.C. 20036
(202) 293-7050

Harold Delaney, Executive Vice-President
Committee on Communications Technology
American Association of State Colleges and Universities
One Dupont Circle, Suite 700
Washington, D.C. 20036
(202) 293-7070

Susan Fratkin, Director of Special Programs
Task Force on Educational Communications
National Association of State Universities and Land-Grant Colleges
One Dupont Circle, Suite 710
Washington, D.C. 20036
(202) 293-7120

Center for Telecommunications Studies
Division of Continuing Education
George Washington University
Washington, D.C. 20052
(202) 676-7062

Harvard Graduate School of Education, Gutman Library
Appian Way
Cambridge, Mass. 02138
(617) 495-4225

Carol Katzki, Associate Director
National University Continuing Education Association
One Dupont Circle
Washington, D.C. 20036
(202) 659-3130

Project on Information Technology and Education
1001 Connecticut Avenue, N.W.
Washington, D.C. 20036
(202) 463-0747

Telecourse and Audio and Radio Course Information

Adult Learning Service, Public Broadcasting Service
475 L'Enfant Plaza, S.W.
Washington, D.C. 20024
(202) 488-5360

Corporation for Public Broadcasting
Annenberg/CPB Project
1111 16th Street, N.W.
Washington, D.C. 20036
(202) 293-6160

Brian Brightly, Adult Learning Listening Network
c/o National Public Radio
2025 M Street, N.W.
Washington, D.C. 20036
(202) 822-2693

Cable Information

Cable Television Information Center
1800 N. Kent Street, Suite 1007
Arlington, Va. 22209
(703) 528-6846

National Federation of Local Cable Programmers
906 Pennsylvania Avenue, S.E.
Washington, D.C. 20003
(202) 544-7272

National Cable Television Association
1724 Massachusetts Avenue, N.W.
Washington, D.C. 20036
(202) 775-3550

Computer Consortia

EDUCOM
P.O. Box 364
Princeton, N.J. 08540
(609) 734-1915

CONDUIT
University of Iowa
P. O. Box 388
Iowa City, Iowa 52244
(319) 353-5789

Video Teleconferencing

ACSN The Learning Channel
1200 New Hampshire Avenue, N.W., Suite 240
Washington, D.C. 20036
(202) 331-8100

National University Teleconference Network
204 Whitehurst
Stillwater, Okla. 74078
(405) 624-6606

Public Service Satellite Consortium
1660 L Street, N.W., Suite 907
Washington, D.C. 20036

CONFERSAT
Public Broadcasting Service
465 L'Enfant Plaza, S.W.
Washington, D.C. 20024
(202) 488-5084

Audio Teleconferencing

Center for Interactive Programs
University of Wisconsin Extension
975 Observatory Drive
Old Radio Hall
Madison, Wis. 53706
(608) 262-4342

Teletext and Videotext

Alternate Media Center
New York University
725 Broadway, Fourth Floor
New York, N.Y. 10003
(212) 598-2852

Videodisk

Nebraska Videodisc Design/Production Group
P.O. Box 8311
Lincoln, Nebr. 68501
(402) 472-3611

Periodicals

Current
Current Publishing Committee
P.O. Box 53358
Washington, D.C. 20009

Educational and Industrial Television
Charles S. Tepfer Publishing, Inc.
51 Sugar Hollow Road
Danbury, Conn. 06180

Educational Technology
Educational Technology Publications, Inc.
140 Sylvan Avenue
Englewood Cliffs, N.J. 07632

Electronic Learning
Scholastic, Inc.
50 West Forty-Fourth Street
New York, N.Y. 10036

ETV Newsletter
Charles S. Tepfer Publishing, Inc.
51 Sugar Hollow Road
Danbury, Conn. 06180

Journal of Educational Technology Systems
Baywood Publishing Co., Inc.
120 Marine Street
Farmingdale, N.Y. 11735

Telescan
American Association for Higher Education
One Dupont Circle, Suite 600
Washington, D.C. 20036

T.H.E. Journal
Information Synergy, Inc.
P.O. Box 17239
Irvine, Calif. 92713

Videodisc/Videotext
Microform Review, Inc.
520 Riverside Avenue
Westport, Conn. 06880

Books

American Association for Higher Education. *New Technologies for Higher Education.* Current Issues in Higher Education, No. 5. Washington, D.C.: American Association for Higher Education, 1981.

Carpenter, T. *Calling the Tune: Communication Technology for Working, Learning, and Living.* Washington, D.C.: National Institute for Work and Learning, 1980.

Communications Technology in Education and Training. Silver Spring, Md.: Information Dynamics, 1982.

Dirr, P., Katz, J., and Pedone, R. *Higher Education Utilization Study.* Washington, D.C.: Corporation for Public Broadcasting, 1981.

Office of Technology Assessment, U.S. Congress. *Informational Technology and Its Impact on American Education.* Washington, D.C.: U.S. Government Printing Office, 1982.

Knapper, C. K. (Ed.). *Expanding Learning Through New Communications Technologies.* New Directions for Teaching and Learning, no. 9. San Francisco: Jossey-Bass, 1982.

Kressel, M. (Ed.). *Adult Learning and Public Broadcasting.* Washington, D.C.: American Association for Community and Junior Colleges, 1983.

Lewis, R. J. *Meeting Learners' Needs Through Telecommunications: A Directory and Guide to Programs.* Center for Learning and Telecommunications, Washington, D.C.: 1983.

The Communications Revolution and the Education of Americans, New Rochelle, N.Y.: Change Magazine Press, 1980.

The Low Power Television Guidebook. Corporation for Public Broadcasting, Washington, D.C., 1980.

McCredie, J. W. *Campus Computing Strategies.* Bedford, Mass.: Digital Press, 1983.

Moss, M. (Ed.). *Telecommunications and Productivity.* Reading, Mass.: Addison-Wesley, 1981.

Parker, L. A., and Olgren, C. H. (Eds.). *Teleconferencing and Electronic Communications.* Madison: Center for Interactive Programs, University of Wisconsin Extension, 1982.

Professional Development and Educational Technology. Washington, D.C.: Association for Educational Communications and Technology, 1980.

Technology and Education. Washington, D.C.: Institute for Educational Leadership, 1981.

Teleguide: A Handbook for Video Teleconference Planners. Washington, D.C.: Public Service Satellite Consortium, 1981.

Yarrington, R. (Ed.). *Using Mass Media for Learning.* Washington, D.C.: American Association of Community and Junior Colleges, 1979.

Pamela J. Tate is associate director of the Compact for Lifelong Educational Opportunities (CLEO) and needs assessment consultant to the Adult Learning Listening Network, a new organization supported by National Public Radio and the Corporation for Public Broadcasting.

Marilyn Kressel is director of the American Association for Higher Education's Center for Learning and Telecommunications.

Index

STATEMENT OF OWNERSHIP, MANAGEMENT, AND CIRCULATION
(Required by 39 U.S.C. 3685)

1. Title of Publication: New Directions for Higher Education. A. Publication number: USPS 990-880. 2. Date of filing: September 30, 1983. 3. Frequency of issue: quarterly. A. Number of issues published annually: four. B. Annual subscription price: $35 institutions; $21 individuals. 4. Location of known office of publication: 433 California Street, San Francisco (San Francisco County), California 94104. 5. Location of the headquarters or general business offices of the publishers: 433 California Street, San Francisco (San Francisco County), California 94104. 6. Names and addresses of publisher, editor, and managing editor: publisher— Jossey-Bass Inc., Publishers, 433 California Street, San Francisco, California 94104; editor—Martin Kramer, 2807 Shasta Rd., Berkeley, CA 94708; managing editor—Allen Jossey-Bass, 433 California Street, San Francisco, California 94104. 7. Owner: Jossey-Bass Inc., Publishers, 433 California Street, San Francisco, California 94104. 8. Known bondholders, mortgages, and other security holders owning or holding 1 percent or more of total amount of bonds, mortgages, or other securities: same as No. 7. 10. Extent and nature of circulation: (Note: first number indicates the average number of copies of each issue during the preceding twelve months; the second number indicates the actual number of copies published nearest to filing date.) A. Total number of copies printed (net press run): 1589, 1605. B. Paid circulation, 1) Sales through dealers and carriers, street vendors, and counter sales: 85, 40. 2) Mail subscriptions: 512, 512. C. Total paid circulation: 597, 552. D. Free distribution by mail, carrier, or other means (samples, complimentary, and other free copies): 125, 125. E. Total distribution (sum of C and D): 772, 677. F. Copies not distributed, 1) Office use, left over, unaccounted, spoiled after printing: 867, 928. 2) Returns from news agents: 0, 0. G. Total (sum of E, F1, and 2—should equal net press run shown in A): 1589, 1605. I certify that the statements made by me above are correct and complete.

JOHN R. WARD
Vice-President